Mary Russell Oleson

# KABUKI

# KABUKI

*by*

YONEZO HAMAMURA
TAKASHI SUGAWARA
JUNJI KINOSHITA
HIROSHI MINAMI

*Edited by*
The Society of Traditional Arts

*Under the Auspices of*
The Institute of the Pacific

*Translated by*
FUMI TAKANO
Associate Professor, Tsuda College

TOKYO
KENKYUSHA LTD

*Manufactured in Japan. Set and Printed by*
THE KENKYUSHA PRESS, *Tokyo*

# Foreword

The Institute of the Pacific was first organized in May 1937 for the purpose of promoting friendly relations among the peoples around the Pacific. It has dedicated itself to scientific research and has published over one hundred books of academic nature. These were all published in Japanese, with only one exception. Although these books were quite favorably received at home, they fell short of our ultimate aim which was to publish books of enduring value in English so as to introduce our life and culture to the world and help increase real understanding of our people among our neighbors across the ocean. This, we thought, would contribute to the cause of peace.

Now it is with a genuine pleasure and satisfaction that at long last we present a phase of our life in English. The *Kabuki* is distinctly a Japanese cultural product and portrays the life, morals and emotions of the Japanese common people in the medieval period, which still has great bearing upon contemporary Japan. An adequate explanation of the *Kabuki* has been overdue. The color prints of Japan have been exported and appreciated in the past one hundred years.

But the Japanese plays and actors, their most important subject matters, have been left unexplained.

The Institute asked and got the consent of four prominent writers who are all authorities in the *Kabuki* to undertake the long needed introduction of the *Kabuki* to the outside world. They collaborated for three years and the result is the present book. The Institute is very grateful to these men of letters for their unstinted labor and untiring effort. As regards the nature of the work the book will speak for itself. We hope this will furnish another link between the people of Japan and those across the seas.

We must also express our warmest gratitude for the patient and conscientious cooperation of Mrs. Fumi Takano who has been responsible for most of the translation from the Japanese, Miss Yukiko Fujita, who took minutes of the authors' meetings and collected necessary materials for the book, and Mr. Masaki Kawaguchi, from whom we received much help in our translation. The translation was carefully gone over by Mrs. Allen Cole to whom we owe sincere appreciation. Last but not least, thanks are due to Mr. Kurōemon Onoe, a prominent *Kabuki* actor, who gave us many valuable suggestions.

YUSUKE TSURUMI

THE INSTITUTE OF THE PACIFIC, TOKYO
MAY 10, 1956

*Collaborators in the present work :*

YONEZO HAMAMURA : born in Tokyo, 1890 ; studied English literature at Waseda University; became an apprentice-student of the Kabuki Playwrights' Room of the Kabuki Theatre in Tokyo, 1911 ; was appointed chief of the Literary Department of the Imperial Theatre of Tokyo, 1921 ; was adviser to the Toho Theatrical Company, 1931–1932 ; was lecturer at the Japan Actors' School founded by Kikugoro VI, 1930–1937. Present positions : Management Committee of the Piccadilly Experimental Theatre of Tokyo; director of the Japan Dramaturgical Society ; member of the Board of Councillors of the Japan Center of the International Theatre Association. Publications : *Kan-i naru Kokugekishi* (A Short History of the Japanese Theatre) ; *Kabuki no Mikata* (How to Appreciate the Kabuki) ; *Kabuki Kyōshitsu* (Lectures on the Kabuki).

TAKASHI SUGAWARA : born in Tokyo, 1903 ; graduated from Keio University, 1925 ; studied at Columbia University, N.Y.C., U.S.A., 1925–1927 ; visited England before returning to Japan; toured in U.S.A. and Europe, 1929–30. Present positions : member of the Management Committees of Nippon Drama Association, of the Piccadilly Experimental Theatre, and of the National Theatre of Japan. Direction and Translation : *Porgy*, *The Voice of the Turtle*, *Death of a Salesman*, *Arsenic and Old Lace*, etc.

JUNJI KINOSHITA: born in Tokyo, 1914; attended a student conference in U.S.A., 1936; graduated from Tokyo University (major: English literature), 1939; was lecturer at Hosei University, 1940–1944. Present position: Professor of dramatics, Meiji University. Plays: *Yūzuru* (Twilight Crane); *Kaeru Shōten* (The Ascension of a Frog); *Minwageki Shū* (Plays Based on Folk-Tales), etc. Translation: *Othello*, W. Somerset Maugham's *Our Betters, For Services Rendered*, etc.

HIROSHI MINAMI, Ph. D.: born in Tokyo, 1914; graduated from Kyoto University (major: psychology), 1940; studied in the U.S.A., 1940–1946; Ph. D., Cornell University, 1943. Present position: Associate Professor, Hitotsubashi University. Publications: *Social Psychology*, 1949. Articles in English: " Social Psychology of Post War Japan," (*Annals of Hitotsubashi University*, 1950); " Human relations in the Japanese Society, (*Ibid.*, Vol. IV, No. 2, 1954).

# *Contents*

## List of Photographs

# Photographs

*by courtesy of*
## MR. IHEE KIMURA

# Photographs

*by courtesy of*
## MR. IHEE KIMURA

The Kabuki Theatre

**Takiyasha Hime** A courtesan in a dance drama. In the right is seen an ancient lighting called *sashidashi*, which is held by a *kōken*. The picture shows an old-style usage of the *hanamichi*. The actor is Nakamura Utaemon (an *onnagata*).

**Michiyuki** Lovers speaking of love as they elope. Mitsuuji (Ichikawa Ebizō) and Tasogare (Onoe Baikō—an *onnagata*).

**Kamisuki** Men often have troubles they cannot confide. The woman, combing her husband's hair, laments and says: "Why must you hide it from me?" Shadows of poverty haunt the scene. Inagawa, the *sumōtori* (wrestler) (Matsumoto Kōshirō), his wife Otome (Nakamura Tokizō—an *onnagata*).

**Nureba**   The *nureba* in the *Kabuki* is often extremely grotesque and erotic; but the scene in this picture is an ordinary love-scene of a comparatively new play, full of the atmosphere of everyday life.   Naozamurai (Ichimura Uzaemon XV), Michitose (Kataoka Nizaemon XII).

***Yusuriba*** Two *chūgen* (footmen) about to extort money from a dry-goods dealer. The character in front, dressed like a woman, is really a man, Benten Kozō (Onoe Kikugorō), the other, Nangō Rikimaru (Nakamura Kichiemon).

***Tachimawari*** (A fight)  A *Kabuki* fight has its own unique style. The picture shows a graceful fight of a *wakashugata* (a young boy in the *Kabuki* plays) in the center, who is Benten Kozō (Onoe Kikugorō).

**KAGAMIJISHI** A dance drama. A lion swirling his mane as he frolics. (Onoe Kikugorō).

**SANBASŌ** An old ceremonial dance, adapted from the *Noh*, to pray for peace and plenty. The actor is Bandō Mistugorō, one of the most outstanding dancers in recent years.

*DŌJŌJI* A dance piece, expressing fully and freely a young girl's emotions of love. She dances over an hour almost entirely by herself. Hanako (Onoe Kikugorō).

***KOTOBUKI SOGA NO TAIMEN*** A most popular historial play, showing unique vigorous acting, called *aragoto*. The play created in the Edo theatres in the 17th century was regularly included, in Edo, in the New Year's program. There are many variations of this *Kyōgen*, as the audience could not be satisfied with exact repetitions every year. Left to right : Asahina (Bandō Mitsugorō), Soga no Gorō (Onoe Kikugorō), Soga no Jūrō (Ichimura Uzaemon).

**SUKEROKU**   Sukeroku (Ichimura Uzaemon) and courtesans. (*Cf.* Chap. II).

**DOMOMATA** A historical *sewamono*, containing the attractions of both the historical play and the *sewamono*. This play was adapted from a *Ningyō Jōruri* play, and is often referred to also as a *gidayī mono*. It is based on a play written by Chikamatsu Monzaemon, the greatest Japanese verse dramatist. Domomata in front (Onoe Kikugorō).

**The "under-the-floor" scene of *SENDAIHAGI*.** The following ten pictures are arranged to show the stage mechanism of the *Kabuki*. The play is *Kyara Sendaihagi* (or *Meiboku Sendaihagi*), centered around the troubles of a *daimyō* family, whose infant lord is exposed to conspiracies. The faithful nurse has to do all the cooking herself for the lord in their living-room, as food prepared in the kitchen may be poisoned. Understanding the situation, the infant lord makes his touching speech: "A *daimyō* is not hungry even if his stomach is empty." That speech used to move all the women spectators to tears, but the present-day young girls sit unmoved; some of them even go on chewing gum! However that may be, unless the actor playing the nurse's part is a great actor, the cooking-scene can be perfectly flat. The first picture in the series shows the scene immediately following the cooking-scene, which has taken place in the inner room hidden now behind the bamboo-screens. The floor of the palace has already been raised a little. The curved line seen in front of the palace shows the edge of the revolving stage. *Kurogo*, holding up a crimson blanket, hide the trap-door, out of which the faithfull retainer Arajishi Otokonosuke is to rise, as the whole palace gradually rises, and the scene changes into the "under-the-floor" scene. Otokonosuke holds a huge rat under his foot as he rises, and he engages in a heroic *aragoto* with this rat. In contrast with the preceding scene which has taken over an hour, and which may have been monotony itself, this lively scene of a most skilful fight between good and evil takes only about five minutes.

From the *Naraku* below the *hanamichi*, the heroic villain Nikki Danjō is about to rise. Having turned himself into a rat by magic, he has stolen a *renbanjō* (a list of signers to a compact) from the palace. The moment the rat on the stage disappears into the trap-door, Nikki Danjō rises in a smoke onto the *hanamichi*, but until he breaks the spell, he is invisible to Otokonosuke, who gnashes his teeth in rage at the thought of having let the villain escape.

After the curtain is drawn across the stage, Nikki Danjō breaks the spell, and walking calmly down the *hanamichi*, he disappears behind the *agemaku*. Otokonosuke (Ichimura Uzaemon XVII), Danjō (Onoe Shōroku).

'Jinya no Ba" Act III, Scene iii o. *ICHINOTANI FUTABA GUNKI,* which was the last scene written by Namiki Sōsuke (1695–1751) before his death. The scene is preceded in the same Act, by "Kojirō Senjin" (Kojirō Leading the Van) and "Kumiuchi" (A Grapple). Nakamura Kichiemon, who is playing Kumagai in these pictures, was a tragedian particularly skilful in playing brave heroes of historical plays. Though he had always been sickly and very thin, once he got on the stage, he turned into a great valiant hero, which showed how truly talented he was. No one equalled him in the mournful and yet powerful speeches. The other major characters are : Yoshitsune (Kōshirō), Midaroku (Ennosuke), Fuji-no-Kata (Sōjūrō), Sagami (Utaemon), Gunji (Matagorō). On the stage stands a young cherry-tree, symbolizing the theme of the play ; and under the tree stands the notice-board. In the first picture, Kumagai has just returned from a visit to a temple, and is met at the gate by Gunji and Sagami. In the second picture, Kumagai glancing back at his wife, whom he has not expected to find there, prepares himself for the inevitable scene to follow. It is what connoisseurs call a vital moment. The third picture shows the stage-hands promptly removing the gate when it is no longer needed.

The fourth picture shows Fuji-no-Kata drawing her sword to attack Kumagai, who has just told Sagami that he has killed Atsumori. Kumagai pacifies the women by speaking to them of the nature of wars.

Then he prepares to go to Yoshitsune's camp for the commander to identify the head. The two women beg him to let them have one look at the head.

In the eighth picture, Yoshitsune, the commander, has appeared from an inner room, and proposes to identify the head here in Kumagai's own camp. When the lid of the head-case is lifted, Kojirō's head is disclosed. Sagami bursts into tears.

Midaroku who has been arrested is also brought in. Yoshitsune knowing that he is a warrior of the enemy clan in disguise, presents him with a case of armor, which contains Atsumori, the enemy prince. Yoshitsune has remembered how he had been rescued by this man years ago when he was a child.

Kumagai, having tasted to the full the bitterness and agony of war, becomes a Buddhist priest
The last picture shows Kichiemon at the climax of his art of expression. The silent *hanamichi*,
as Kumagai walks away, turns into a veritable path of life which human sorrows must tread.

# KABUKI

# Chapter  I
# A Visit to the Kabuki Theatre

We are now going to the *Kabuki* Theatre, located in downtown Tokyo, to see a performance of the *Kabuki*. The Theatre was damaged during the recent war, but it was restored in January, 1951, and is now a playhouse of three galleries with a seating capacity of 2,600. It is a Western-style building, with some features of Japanese medieval architecture. As an example of architecture it is of no particular merit, but it has one feature which is decidedly unique—namely, the actor's passage, which is about four feet wide and about level with the eyes of the audience on the first floor, projecting at right angles from the left hand side of the stage and running clear through the pit. This is the *hanamichi* —the " flower path." At the other end—the far end from the stage—this " flower path " is connected to a small green-room, partitioned from the audience by means of a curtain (the *agemaku*). The Kabuki drama is always a cooperative product of the performers and the audience. The persistent, and in a sense pathetic, existence of this " flower path " shows how the endless progress and refinement of the *Kabuki* has depended on the collaboration and sympathy of the audience.* The difficulty of the language may sometimes make the performances seem tedious, but patience will bring ample reward.

Now the sound of clappers announcing the beginning of the play is heard. The *hyōshigi* (wooden clappers) consist of a pair of sticks made of oak, each one foot long. Clapping the *hyōshigi* is considered one of the important tasks of the stage director, and there are rigorous rules regulating it. The manner of clapping differs with the contents of the play. The clapping serves instantly to direct the attention of the audience to the stage where the play is about to begin. Then the characteristically oriental sound of gongs and drums is heard. The gongs and drums indicate that the scene we are to see is one of a battlefield. The famous play *Ichinotani Futaba Gunki* is about to begin. The theme of this play concerns the strife for power that took place between the Genji and the Heike, two great military

---

* The strip-tease show which has enjoyed great popularity in post war Japan makes use of an apron-stage which is but a degenerated *hanamichi*. And in order to please the taste of the masses, " beauties " are made to bathe in a bath-tub placed upon it. If this is the new " flower path " devised by our contemporary show managements, they have only to be ashamed before the original creators of the *hanamichi* centuries ago. This single example of misuse of the " flower way " reveals how incompetent the modern Japanese people are to operate the great vehicle of the *Kabuki*. And that is one reason why the *Kabuki* should be seen with an unspoiled eye.

clans in medieval Japan. Louder becomes the sound
of the instruments that are hidden behind the small
wooden house, with a grated window, situated to
the left (from the andience) of the proscenium. This
orchestrabox of the *Kabuki* is a veritable treasure-
house of all kinds of oriental musical instruments.

As the clapping of *hyōshigi*, heard in between
the accompanying music, now quickens its tempo
and rises to a crescendo, the curtain is pulled aside,
horizontally, from left to right. The stage is empty.
The lights over the heads of the audience do not
go out; in fact, the audience's seats are kept as
bright as the stage itself. On the stage you see, to
the right, a simple black wooden gate, and in the
center a painted fence of logs. That the stage is
illumined so brightly all over, notwithstanding the
fact that the action takes place during the hours
from midnight to daybreak, is of course in com-
pliance with the traditions of the classical play.

As soon as the percussion instruments subside,
the *gidayū* music pours out from behind the blinded
window of an elevated structure in the right hand
corner of the stage. *Gidayū* is a form of narrative
ballad accompanied by the *samisen*, a typical Japanese
stringed instrument. Not a few Westerners with
sensitive ears have been appalled by the hoarse,
strained voice of the *gidayū* reciter, and some have
humorously described it as the gasping of a strangled

rooster. No, *gidayū* can hardly claim much musical beauty. Music of this type has its origin in the tunes with which Buddhist scriptures were read in the remote past. This narrative singing of ancient times developed into various classes of narrative ballad in the medieval period, and was brought to perfection in more recent times by the plebeian class. It is natural, therefore, to hear in *gidayū* the sighs and wails of the people, for *gidayū* is nothing more than the prayers of man forever wandering between the worlds of gods and beasts. It is also to be remembered that *gidayū* is a creation by a people who knew no science. One should accept it as such, even if it is a little unpalatable, for this " narrative singing," laden with both musical and unmusical sounds, is still capable of conveying to us a poignant message as it undulates and intertwines.

In the meantime, the *gidayū* music has come to a temporary pause, and a handsome youth in armor is now to appear on the stage via the *hanamichi*. Japanese armor of the civil war period is quite unique; it is distinctly different from that of the West. On the *Kabuki* stage it is beautified with a great richness of color. The metal parts are painted all over, and decorated with silk threads. It is noteworthy that the colors of the armor used in the *Kabuki* are meant to suggest the character of the wearer in the play. In the present case the color is pink, symbolizing youth. The wearer of this armor is Kojirō, the only son of General Kumagai, the hero of the play. The appearance of an actor brings forth enthusiastic shouting from the audience, expressing their encouragement and expectation. Cries like "*Mattemashita*" (lit. "I have been waiting,") and "*Daitōryō*" (lit. "Great leader,") uttered at the right moment are highly effective in increasing the excitement of the entire audience.

The lights are concentrated upon one spot on the *hanamichi* called *shichi-san* (lit. "seven-three")—a spot three-tenths of the distance from the main stage. The curtain of the small green-room at the far end of the *hanamichi* is pulled aside with a swishing sound behind the audience, which serves as a signal for the connoisseurs among the audience to shout to the entering actor his stage name. At the same time, a man in black, seated at the right front edge of the stage, strikes a pair of clappers against the wooden board placed in front of him, using the two clappers alternately. This serves to emphasize the manliness of the actor, who now comes running on the scene, and at the same time to represent the sound of running footsteps. Accompanied by the piercing sound of the clappers, the actor makes his way amid the audience. Responding to their cheers, Kojirō begins his monologue on the *hanamichi*. "This is my first battle," he says, "but since nobody seems to have arrived before me, I will dash into the enemy camp and win fame for myself." So saying, he proceeds to the main stage, and looks into the camp. He makes an exaggerated pose called *miye*.*

From within the gate comes the sound of *gagaku*, a type of music preserved in the Imperial Court since the eighth century. Kojirō listens intently, and is struck by the elegance of town-dwellers who, unlike country warriors like himself, do not forget music even on the battle-field. Then a fellow soldier, Hirayama, appears at the left-hand side of the stage and urges Kojirō to go onward. Finally the young warrior announces himself in a loud voice, and runs into the enemy camp. Hirayama, who is left behind, strains his ears to find out what is happening within.

At this moment, Kumagai, the hero of this play, makes his grand appearance by way of the *hana-michi*. He is clad in black armor, which symbolizes strength. Again cheers rise from the audience. On being told by Hirayama that Kojirō has broken into the enemy camp all by himself, Kumagai rattles his armor and darts through the gate. All at once, clamors are heard within the camp. Hirayama walks up and down, not knowing what to do. Soon

---

* *Miye* is a pose intended to create a strong impression of the action. It is a technique similar to the " close-up " used in movies. *Miye* is made in most cases by a single actor, but sometimes more than two actors will make a *miye* at the end of an act, so that the stage as a whole presents a picture-effect. *Miye* is one of the features best characterizing the *Kabuki*.

Kumagai comes out of the gate, carrying Kojirō in his arms. He tells Hirayama that he is going to take his wounded son back to his camp to look after him, and goes off by way of the *hanamichi*. Thereupon, enemy soldiers swarm out of the gate with loud war-cries and surround Hirayama. Here a sound of the clappers is heard, and with that as a signal the stage begins to revolve, taking the play into the Second Scene.

The stage is again empty at the beginning of Scene II. We are on the beaches of Suma. The background has a twofold formation: the rear part shows a distant view of the sea, and the forward part, consisting of stylized waves made of canvas, lies low on the stage.* On these canvas waves floats a vessel—the flag-ship of the enemy's fleet, the deck of which is covered with brocade curtains —all made of paper. Presently *gidayū* music resumes its wailing notes.** Although these events have been introduced here one by one, they are observed simultaneously the moment the revolving stage

* This change of scene is effected under the same bright illumination, exposing to the audience's view part of the back-stage mechanism and stage hands. This partial exposure of the stage mechanism serves to remind the audience that the play is an art and not life, a presentation rather than a representation of life.

** All the speeches and movements of the actors are guided as well as explained by *gidayu* music. The *Kabuki* is both a musical drama and a quasi-ballet; for it is richly embellished with the music of gongs, drums, etc.; and poses and movements are characteristically exaggerated.

has stopped its rotation at the proper position.

There now appears on the scene, via the *hana-michi*, a princess, young and delicate, and totally out of place in these bloody surroundings. She is clad in a vermilion costume embroidered with gold, silver and many-colored threads. The long robe which trails around her completely hides her feet. The part of the princess is being played by a type of actor known as *oyama* who specializes in women's roles. One finds it difficult to believe that the part is being played by a man, so perfectly feminine does the princess appear to be. Indeed, the *oyama* epitomizes the art of the *Kabuki*. This princess is Lady Tamaori, betrothed to Atsumori, an enemy of Kumagai.

We have already learned in Scene I that the enemy forces were attacked by Kumagai, Hirayama and others. Foreseeing a defeat, the enemy commanding unit has already relinquished the land, and fled far into the offing in a vessel. The princess, however, having lost sight of Atsumori in the turmoil of the battle, has been wandering helplessly in search of him. Now Hirayama enters from the right hand side of the stage, espies the approaching princess, and puts on a devilish grin, for he has long been looking for a chance to make love to her. He seizes her by the arm and tries to seduce her, but finding her unassailable, he fells her with a sword.

At this moment, war-cries are heard nearby, and Hirayama makes a hasty exit to the left.

By this time the vessel on the sea has sailed to the right and disappeared. Then, with the sound of the clappers, the background splits into two parts, one part withdrawing to the right and the other to the left, revealing now the view of the more distant sea. At the same time, two more sets of canvas waves are added to those already on the stage, a low one being placed in front and a tall one in the rear of the original, so that one sees waves at three different distances. The vessel of the former scene appears from the right hand side and floats over the farthest canvas waves. The rolling of a big drum imitating the sound of the waves is heard. Then enters via the *hanamichi* Atsumori, mounted on a white horse. He wears a gorgeous scarlet-threaded armor giving a general color impression of pink. He, too, has foreseen a defeat and has come thus far following the movement of his retreating unit.

The horse he is riding is not of course a real horse. Its body is a *papier-mâché* work, made to look as real as possible, and contains in it two experienced actors, each of whom wears a pair of tight trousers painted in the likeness of a horse's legs. The fore legs of this horse are rather convincingly real because they bend backward as a real

horse's do, but the hind-legs—it is only natural—
bend backward, too, which live horse's legs could
never do. This is strange to anyone's eye, but as
the play goes on this man-horse begins to appear
real enough; in fact, it is more convincing than a
real horse would be here. That, one might say, is
the magic of the *Kabuki*.*

Atsumori, who has by this time reached the
main stage on horse-back, disappears to the right
but reappears immediately and rides to the left,
taking his course between the first and the second
canvas-work waves. He is supposed to be wading
through the shallow water. His horse, from the
body down, is hidden behind the foremost waves
and his action looks as if he were wading through
water. Finally he disappears to the left. The next
moment a child-actor dressed as Atsumori, mounted
on a smaller horse, appears from the left and marches
between the second and the third canvas-work waves.
This is to show that Atsumori has now waded a long
way into the sea. When this little Atsumori has
reached the center of the stage, Kumagai appears on
the *hanamichi*, mounted on a black horse, shouting at
the top of his voice.

As Kumagai does not wear a helmet at this time,

* Unfortunately, however, not more than two such veteran " horses "
are available today in Japan. More-over, the " forelegs " of one of them
has recently quit the thankless job and become a grocer. When his help
is indispensable he must be coaxed back temporarily to the stage.

it is a good chance to observe the unique make-up used in the *Kabuki*. The entire face is painted in light pink, and one strong line in red is drawn from the outer corner of each eye to the forehead. This line is called the *kumadori*. It is sometimes said to be taken from the make-up used in the Chinese drama, but it is also sometimes said that it has its origin in the *Noh* masks. However that may be, the *kumadori* serves to remind one of the swelling up of muscles and blood-vessels that accompany the outbursts of strong emotions. The tips of the hair on the wig worn by Kumagai are curled up like a lion's mane. This wig is used exclusively for this scene.

Now Kumagai, hailing Atsumori in a loud voice, comes onto the stage, where he rides in a large circle two or three times. He then disappears to the right but reappears shortly and wades in the shallow water, as Atsumori did a few seconds ago, until he disappears to the left. The child-actor in the role of Atsumori, thus hailed, turns round and faces the front. Presently another child-actor, in the role of Kumagai, appears from the left, and the two confront each other in the center of the stage, a long way from the shore. This is an excellent example of the use of child-actors to create a sense of perspective. The two mounted child-actors cross swords in the sea. It seems a well-matched fight, and finally they grapple with each other on horse back. The wooden clappers are heard and a curtain with waves painted all over it falls swiftly from the ceiling between the first and the second canvas-waves, concealing the distant figures of Kumagai and Atsumori.*

From the orchestra is heard flute music of a quick rhythm, and the white horse which, in the previous scene, carried Atsumori appears from the right, with no rider, runs crazily past the wave curtain, and goes away via the *hanamichi*. When the horse has disappeared, the wave-curtain drops to the floor and is dragged out to the left of the stage. Now the background is the open sea, without vessels or anything. In the foreground stand the first canvas waves only, the second and the third having been withdrawn. Now there enter two stage-men in black —called *kurogo* (lit. " black clothes ")—holding a big scarlet blanket, each by an upper corner, and they stand in the middle of the stage. Their action may remind one of a juggler who flaps a handkerchief over and over with his hands to show that it conceals no secret. In this case, however, the scarlet blanket indicates that something very important is to follow. At length, the men in black retire with

* This type of curtain smaller than the proscenium of the stage is a device frequently used in the *Kabuki* drama for a change of scene. If the curtain is black, it is supposed to indicate either " night" or " non-existence of objects "; if blue, "noon " or " the sky." In the present case, the curtain has waves painted on it because the scene is of the sea.

the blanket.

You see now in the middle of the stage Kumagai and Atsumori rising slowly from beneath by means of a special elevator. The two warriors do not move at all. They are frozen in their position with the former holding the latter to the ground. This kind of appearance is technically called *seridashi* (push-up). The actors are raised from the cellar below in certain fixed poses. This, of course, is done by the elevator which exposes first the face, then the body, and finally the legs. The actors, in a fixed pose, make their appearance without batting an eyelash, like a group of dolls, accompanied by music coming from the window in the left corner of the stage. Here Kumagai and Atsumori appear from below frozen at the climax of their mortal fight. It is all far beyond logic or reality.

When they are level with the stage, Atsumori, the young enemy general, rises to his feet, and tells Kumagai that he is Atsumori, only son of Taira-no Tsunemori, and calmly asks him to cut off his head. Kumagai, however, is touched by the delicate beauty of the boy, which might be compared to a flower not yet in bloom. Kumagai, unable to bring himself to kill the boy, advises him to leave the place immediately. But this is overheard by Hirayama, who is half seen at the farthest end of the *hanamichi* where there is supposed to be a small hill. Hirayama loudly reviles Kumagai, asking him if he means to release an enemy general after once catching him. Finding himself thus compelled, Kumagai finally beheads Atsumori, much against his will; and, in order to dispel the suspicion of his fellow soldiers, he strains his sorrow-stricken voice to announce that he has killed Atsumori, the enemy general.

Hearing this announcement, the mortally-wounded Princess Tamaori creeps out of the bush of reeds at the right, and, explaining that she is betrothed to Atsumori, asks that she might be allowed to have just one look at her dead fiancé's face. But her vision is already failing, and with eyes wide open, she breathes her last. Kumagai is overwhelmed by a sense of the tragedy of war. He takes a shield found near-by, places the corpses of the betrothed couple on it, and sends it floating on the waves.

In the meantime, Kumagai's horse, in anxious search of its master, has popped its head in at the left. What an extraordinary horse, indeed, to have such a sense for drama! But nothing is impossible in the *Kabuki,* and all this comes very naturally in the tragic intensity of Kumagai's emotion which has been played up strongly to this point.

Holding in his left hand Atsumori's head wrapped in cloth, and the horse's rein in his right, Kumagai stands in the middle of the stage, suppressing his tears but too sad to take his steps homeward. All this while the *gidayū* music narrates his fierce sorrow, reiterating his lamentation in heart-rending words. At last, no longer able to control his grief, Kumagai turns his back to the audience and weeps, placing his head upon the neck of his horse. The violent trembling of his shoulders moves the 2,600 people in the theatre who can see only his back. Amid the sound of gongs, drums and the clappers, the curtain falls.

Since on the battlefield it is the duty of a soldier to fight and kill, Kumagai's lamentation on killing Atsumori would seem to be over-exaggerated. Kumagai's lamentation here is as intense as the grief of King Oedipus when he learned that, by a trick of cruel fate, he had married his own mother. What is the reason for this intense grief? That he has had to kill a boy about the same age as his own son Kojirō is not enough to account for it. The answer to this question is given in the next Act.

Act III begins with the scene of General Kumagai's camp. The drum announcing the hour is heard, and, with the sound of wooden clappers, the curtain rises, revealing an open building with a high floor. A flight of three steps leads from the floor down to the garden in the foreground. On the left of the stage stands a wooden gate. This is the typical stage-set for a military camp in a historical play. Outside the gate stands a young cherry-tree in full bloom, beside which is a notice-board stating: "Whoever cuts a branch off this tree shall have one finger cut off his hand." A few villagers come by and stop to read the notice. They walk away whispering to each other, "Oh, this is horrible." Then the small curtain in the right hand corner of the stage is removed, revealing a jutting platform about three feet high, on which sit the *gidayū* reciter and his *samisen* accompanist, who have been supplying the narration from behind the blinded window.

In the meantime, Sagami, wife of Kumagai, enters the room in the building by opening the sliding screens. She has just arrived at this camp, in the absence of her husband, after a long and strenuous trip. She is filled with anxiety about her son Ko-jirō, who is participating in battle for the first time. Temple-bells announce the evening service. Then a voice calls in the small green-room at the rear of the orchestra. "The master's return!" This is followed by the *gidayū* reciter's explanation that Kumagai is returning from a Buddhist service. The man who announced Kumagai's return is one of his retainers. This would perhaps make one wonder whether there is another entrance to the camp. It is not clear, and we have to accept the retainer's announcement as foreshadowing a grave dramatic situation which is to follow after Kumagai's return.

Kumagai, dressed in an ordinary visiting costume

(see Chapter II, p. 32), appears on the *hanamichi*, absorbed in meditation, his head bent forward a little, his arms folded. In his right hand he grips a *juzu* (rosary, i.e. beads strung on a string, like a necklace, used in all Buddhist services). When he has covered two-thirds of the *hanamichi*, another tolling of the bell is heard. He notices that he is almost back at his camp and puts the rosary in his sleeve, though this action may not be noticeable to the audience. He has by now made an important decision. The wig worn by him is now of quite an ordinary kind. His face is painted light pink, and the *kumadori* lines drawn in red from the eye-tails to the forehead are now thinner and shorter. Compared with his make-up in the previous Act, he gives a somewhat quieter impression. Reaching the main stage, Kumagai gazes on the cherry-tree and the notice-board for a moment, standing with his back to the audience, and then enters the garden through the gate. His retainer Gunji appears from the right, and, sitting down by the door-post, he makes Sagami, Kumagai's wife, sit by his side, as if to protect her. Kumagai goes up the steps and takes his seat on the floor without even addressing a word to his wife sitting behind the retainer.

Here the scene-shifters come onto the stage and take away the wooden gate. This by no means implies that the gate has actually disappeared. In-

— 17 —

stead, it is to be understood that henceforward the whole stage will be used as the space inside the house. The actors are now able to move with more freedom. This is one of the established agreements in the appreciation of the *Kabuki* drama, and has the effect of stirring the dramatic imagination of the audience.

The retainer Gunji then informs Kumagai that during his absence Kajiwara (Kumagai's colleague but on ill terms with him) has come to the camp, bringing with him a stone-mason whom he wanted Kumagai to cross-examine, and that Kajiwara is now waiting for him in an inner room. Kumagai sends Gunji in to entertain Kajiwara, then turns to Sagami and asks her why she has come to this bloody battlefield. The wife offers several apologies, and asks if their son Kojirō is doing well. Kumagai answers, in a sturdy tone which conceals his inner disturbances, that Kojirō has been slightly wounded but has distinguished himself at the Battle of Ichinotani by leading the van, while he himself has been able to achieve the greatest fame by killing the enemy general Atsumori. Sagami is struck with horror at these words.

Why is Sagami horror-stricken? Only a short while ago Sagami came to the camp with Atsumori's mother, Fuji-no-Kata, who was being pursued by Kumagai's soldiers, and the old lady is now being kept in the next room. Fuji-no-Kata having heard of the death of her son, has demanded Sagami's help to avenge the murder—namely, to kill Kumagai. Poor Sagami has just been appeasing Fuji-no-Kata, telling her that it must all be founded on some mistake. Fuji-no-Kata is a lady to whom Kumagai and Sagami owe some obligation, for she belongs to their former lord's family.

It is now the husband's turn to be horrified, for just at this moment an elderly lady emerges from the adjacent room, and tries to stab him with a dagger. (A woman of a *samurai* family frequently carried a dagger for self-protection.) In the nick of time, Kumagai catches her by the arm and holds her down. Sagami, in great disconcertion, holds her husband back and discloses to him the identity of the lady. They had not, indeed, seen each other for sixteen years. Kumagai thereupon changes his attitude and tells the lady that on a battlefield one must suppress one's personal feelings and that he had to behead Atsumori.

Here, the exaggerated gestures of the man as he relates the past event strike one as being almost grotesque, for he goes through a long series of *miye*. Both action and speech are boldly magnified. Accompanied by the rhythm of *gidayū* music the actor speaks and dances. It is a "story and action" (*shikatabanashi*) performed simultaneously. Known by the term *monogatari* (story, narrative), it is a unique and extremely difficult form of acting employed in historical *Kabuki* pieces. To do this successfully, it is necessary that the *gidayū* reciter, whose part is similar to that of the chorus in the Greek drama, as well as the *samisen* accompanist, have the power to inspire the actor to go through the act of narrating. If people seeing the *Kabuki* for the first time find it difficult to comprehend it, repeated visits will enable them in time to appreciate the beauty of this typically *Kabuki* acting.

Having finished his long dance narration, Kumagai draws a deep sigh, and tells his wife to take Fuji-no-Kata to some safe place immediately, since no place can be so dangerous a place for her to remain as this camp. So saying Kumagai retires to the inner room. In a short while Kumagai has to show Atsumori's head to the commander Yoshitsune.*

Fuji-no-Kata and Sagami who are left to themselves in the room look at each other. Gongs for the evening service are heard far and near in the camp, and the two women gaze with heavy hearts on the torch lights twinkling in the numerous camps around the place. Choking with tears, Fuji-no-Kata takes out the "Flute of the Green Leaves" (*Aoba no Fue*), a memento of Atsumori, and shows it to Sagami. On

---

* One will notice that, as he rises to leave, the sliding screens open by themselves without his lifting a finger. This miracle is of course effected by the men in black—the *kurogo*. In this scene one sees so many of these men in black scurrying all over the stage, achieving many such miracles, that they will be distracting at first, but in time one comes to ignore them.

her way to this camp she bought this flute from a stone-mason in the village of Suma. (The stone-mason had been entrusted with the keeping of the flute by Atsumori's ghost who came to order a tombstone for himself. Tradition has it that Atsumori was an excellent flute player). Sagami then suggests that Fuji-no-Kata play a tune on the flute as a memorial service, as its exquisite sound will comfort the departed soul. Fuji-no-Kata agrees and begins to play. As she plays, a strange shadow appears on the *shōji* (paper-screen) at the right. "Is this Atsumori, my son?" the lady cries, and running to the *shōji*, flings it open, only to find a set of scarlet-braided armor and helmet placed on a case.

Kumagai reappears at the center, carrying the "head case" (*kubi-oke*) containing Atsumori's decapitated head. Seeing this, the two women cling to Kumagai from both sides, and Sagami beseeches him to allow Fuji-no-Kata one look at the dead man's face. Kumagai, however, refuses, saying that he has no right to do so until he has had it examined by the commander. Tearing himself away from the women he descends the steps and walks briskly in the direction of the *hanamichi*. The sound of a *tsuzumi* (a type of drum peculiar to Japan) is heard at this moment; a voice calls from an inner room at the center, " Here I am, ready to examine the head." General Yoshitsune enters, accompanied by an adjutant.

At this point all the sliding screens of the room are removed, except one pair at the center, and now we see beyond the house the battlefield of Ichinotani extending between the ranges of mountains, where several banners and ensigns typical of medieval Japan are floating in the wind. It is an extremely clumsy painting done in water-color, but when combined with the costumes of the actors in front of it, it produces a singularly agreeable ensemble.

Kumagai, thus accosted, climbs the steps again and takes his seat on the floor. Yoshitsune sits on a kind of folding stool used in military camps, while the adjutant squats cross-legged on the floor. Then Yoshitsune begins in a dignified tone, " Kumagai, you have sent in your resignation when the battle is in full swing. Why is it? I have come thus far wishing to learn what you mean by it. But first let me examine Atsumori's head." Thereupon Kumagai comes out on to the verandah and, stretching out his right arm, pulls up the notice-board standing beside the cherry-tree.* Kumagai then presents the

* Whether Kumagai should pull up the notice-board with his own hand has always been a controversial point, and opinion is still divided. Since the cherry-tree and the notice-board stand outside the camp, Kumagai, however tall he may be, would not be able to reach the board from inside the house. On this ground some critics have suggested that the post be brought to him by those ubiquitous men in black. However, most great actors have pulled it up with their own hands and this has become fixed as a tradition. There are in the Kabuki many such instances of controversy regarding the details of acting.

board to Yoshitsune, declaring that he has decapitated Atsumori according to the instruction in the notice, and asks him to inspect the head. After thus calling the attention of Yoshitsune, Kumagai removes the lid of the case, exposing Atsumori's head. Sagami, who is sitting with others to see it, is manifestly shocked, and moves closer to it, calling out, " That head is . . . ." Fuji-no-Kata also moves toward it, wishing to have one look at her dead son. Kumagai hurriedly puts the lid back, silences Sagami with a motion of his right hand, and, taking the notice-board in his left, pushes back Fuji-no-Kata who clings to him. The man and two women struggle for a moment, before they settle into an artistic composition like a group sculpture. We have now come to the climax of this Act.

After thus struggling on the high floor, Sagami pushed forcibly from behind by Kumagai, totters down the stairs and stops at the left of it. Fuji-no-Kata, who has been holding on to the notice-board, is pulled forward, and she too staggers down the stairs and assumes a position to the right of it. Both the two women turn round and look up at Kumagai, who at this moment comes forward, stands with legs apart on the second step, holds the notice-board upside down on the top step, and, placing his right hand on it, stares fixedly in a *miye*. (He first closes his eyes, then opens them, turning the pupils toward the bridge of his nose.) At the same time, the two women, as though crushed by his stare, fall powerless on the ground, with their faces turned to Kumagai.

Just then, at the extreme right of the stage, the man seated under the platform of the *gidayū* music beats the wooden board before him with the small square wooden sticks in quick tempo. We have already seen a similar practice in Act I, Scene 1.

After this great *miye*, Kumagai once again shows the head of Atsumori to Yoshitsune, who fixes his gaze upon it, and praises Kumagai for the deed. Then Kumagai, in a suddenly lowered voice, urges his wife to show the head to Fuji-no-Kata. The wife nods assent, but she is overwhelmed by tears because the head is not that of Atsumori but of her own son Kojirō.

The " one branch " and the " one finger " mentioned in the notice meant the " one child." Previous to this the commander Yoshitsune, on leaving for Ichinotani battlefield, had handed this notice-board to Kumagai with the injunction that he should jealously guard the young cherry-tree in his camp. Kumagai interpreted this as a command to save by all means the enemy general Atsumori, as young and handsome as a cherry-tree. And, of course, Kumagai's interpretation was correct.

Kumagai had fallen in love with Sagami sixteen

years ago while in court service. But as love affairs were forbidden at court, Kumagai and Sagami would have been punished, had it not been for the kind intervention of Fuji-no-Kata, the wife of their master. They were spared punishment and allowed to leave the palace. It happened that both Fuji-no-Kata and Sagami were expectant mothers at the time. Soon they each had a boy, and the two boys grew up to be fine warriors. These were the circumstances which led to the present tragedy of Kumagai and his wife.

The head we believed to be Atsumori's was not his. The tragedy of sacrificing a member of one's own family as *migawari* (scapegoat) in order to save one's benefactor is often adopted in the *Kabuki*, but in no other case is it elaborated to such an extreme as here. *Ichinotani Futaba Gunki* is almost the only piece among the classical plays of Japan which has an undertone of anti-war sentiments, but it is noteworthy that efforts are made in it to emphasize the tragedy of war in an outlandish and improbable story.

Explanations up to this point have been made at considerable length. A few more details of the play remain. The secret understanding between Kumagai and Yoshitsune to save the life of Atsumori is detected by Kajiwara who eavesdrops in the next room. Kajiwara steals out to report this to the general headquarters. He is followed by the stone-mason, who kills him with the claw of his chisel. This mason, called Midaroku, is a *samurai* in disguise —a well-known warrior, Taira-no Munekiyo, of the Heike clan. Munekiyo had saved Yoshitsune and his mother and his two brothers when Yoshitsune was three years of age. He had never forgotten this favor, and it was partly to requite it that he saved Atsumori's life. Yoshitsune, therefore, presents Midaroku with the armor case containing the person of Atsumori within. The latter accepts it as a plain stone-mason in no way connected with either of the fighting clans of the Genji or the Heike.

Kumagai, who has withdrawn at the command of Yoshitsune to get ready for another campaign, appears at the center for the third time. He is clad in armor and helmet. His wife, Sagami, who is still too deeply grieved to regain composure, wants to know how it was possible to replace Atsumori with Kojirō in the midst of the raging battle. Kumagai explains calmly that the wounded youth whom he had helped back to the camp was Lord Atsumori, and the other youth whom he had called back from the sea and beheaded was Kojirō. But Sagami cannot help regretting her husband's deeds, and asks him if he did not realize Kojirō was his only son. Witnessing this tragic scene, Yoshitsune is moved to tears. But he realizes he is commanding an army; he raises

— 26 —

his voice, and declares that it is time for the expedi-
tion to the west. (The word "west" here is to be
taken to mean the Western Paradise of Buddha).
In response to this Kumagai takes off his helmet,
belt, and armor. He now appears before us with a
tonsured head, wearing the black robe of priesthood.*
His new outfit brings fresh tears to the audience's
eyes. Kumagai, wishing the commander good health,
bids him farewell, and slowly descends the steps
along the left edge. A warrior of unsurpassed valor
only one moment ago, he now looks suddenly emaci-
ated and shortened in stature. This change should
be noted carefully. "If chance allows, let us meet
again," say the women to each other. "If alive,
let us meet again," say the men to each other.
"Take good care of yourself," is the last greeting
Yoshitsune gives Kumagai. Relinquishing fame, his
home, and his beloved wife, with whom he has
shared the hardships of life for so many years, he
leaves the camp, alone.

"Sixteen years. Why, it was but a twinkle of
the eye. It is a dream, alas, a dream." These are
the words that escape the lips of monk Kumagai
as he walks absent-mindedly to the *hanamichi* and
stops there for a moment. He then sits down on
the ground. At this moment, the striped curtain

---

* This total change of costume performed on the stage is a technique
often practised in the *Kabuki*.

(of a type peculiar to the *Kabuki* drama) is drawn from right to left.

A *samisen* player appears on the *hanamichi*. Kumagai rises again to his feet and strikes the floor with his stick. This is followed by quiet music by the *samisen*. In the small green-room at the end of the *hanamichi* gongs and drums are sounded faintly, suggesting the clamor of fighting on the distant battlefield. Hearing this, Kumagai picks up his stick and holds his hat under his left arm, and, with a momentary look of excitement, stands with his legs slightly apart. But he immediately remembers that he has no longer anything to do with war. With drooping head, Kumagai gazes sadly on his stick, then at the main stage. His mind is already made up, and nothing can change it. With his cane in hand, he takes one step, two steps, forward, and then, as if to shake off all haunting memories, he takes his hat in both hands, covers his head with it, and, bending forward, runs into the *agemaku*, the small curtain at the end of the *hanamichi*. The *samisen* has struck its final chord, the wooden clappers are struck, and at long last the play of Kumagai has come to an end.

# Chapter II
# The Esthetics of the Kabuki

The *Kabuki* has always belonged to the common people, who in Japan rose to power at the beginning of the modern era through their financial strength. Their life was soon restricted, however, under the absolute feudal system which was enforced by the warrior class who had held the greatest power in the medieval era. At the same time the freedom to trade and communicate with foreign lands was also suppressed. It meant a literal isolation for Japan: the vast seas surrounding her which should have been roads leading to the ends of the world had, on the contrary, bound Japan within a few small islands cut off from the rest of the world. It meant for the populace loss of opportunities for constructive efforts for invention and creation. Under such conditions was the *Kabuki* produced, into which the people had, within their very limited freedom, poured all their sorrows and their joys. It was, indeed, a drama by the people, for the people, and of the people. It provided them with a dream, a vision, as well as knowledge acquired visually.

The *Kabuki*, therefore, is free, vulgar, and even

picaresque. Some people call it the " art of idiocy." It is also a " flower of evil." Our great scholar of Shakespeare, Dr. Shōyō Tsubouchi, who translated the complete works of Shakespeare, and who was the leader of the modern drama movement in Japan, compared the *Kabuki* to the chimera of Greek mythology. It is, therefore, impossible to define it accurately according to the Western idea of drama, and it is likewise very difficult to explain what exactly the esthetics of the *Kabuki* is. We may only succeed in suggesting a bare outline of the subject. Of the beauty of the *Kabuki*, one aspect which may easily be recognized by anyone is the pictorial effect created on the stage. Also, a play from beginning to end is embellished with music. This music is characteristically oriental, and may sound strange to people who are unfamiliar with it; but throughout the performance it leads the action of the actors and the emotional tone created on the stage. Thus there is the beauty of the music. Thirdly, there is the beauty of the form, of the stylized performance, which it has naturally acquired since it is a great popular drama that has grown, developed, and been refined during four centuries, including the present. We shall now discuss in some detail these three aspects of the *Kabuki*—its pictorial beauty, its musical beauty, and its beauty of form.

Let us begin with the pictorial beauty. This

includes the beauty found in various parts: the setting, properties, the actors' make-up, their wigs, costumes, actions; and then there is the overall artistic effect produced by the combination of all these aspects. But, of course, what attracts our attention first of all is the beauty of the costumes. Nowadays, there is a tendency to use extravagant material and try to produce a dazzling effect; but the real beauty of *Kabuki* costumes is not found in such gay brilliance. The real beauty is found rather in its simplicity which is full of nuances. Although all the costumes are now provided by the company, until about the middle of the nineteenth century, they were provided by each individual actor, at his own expense. Only the costumes for the actors of the lowest ranks were provided by the company.

Thus it was difficult for financial reasons to use good material freely; besides, it was strictly forbidden by the government. The actors, therefore, made untiring efforts to produce costumes that would appear beautiful to the audience, out of odd pieces of silk and cotton. Such conditions naturally helped the creation of beautiful variations and styles in the *Kabuki* costumes. There is a technique called the *hikinuki*, by which one costume is transformed into a different costume, not only once but twice or even three times during the actual performance, in full sight of all the audience. This technique may have been devised originally as a vent for the *Kabuki* actors' anger in not being able to use rich costumes like those of the *Noh* actors, though, of course, what it aimed at was the production of a spectacular effect.

As we have already learned, *Ichinotani Futaba Gunki* is a bloody story of battlefields, and is not therefore a suitable play to explain the pictorial beauty of the *Kabuki*. Still, it has a beauty full of local color peculiar to the historical plays in the *Kabuki*, which is seen, for instance, in the costume of the hero Kumagai. There are two forms of presenting Kumagai, which differ from each other particularly in the main part of the " Jinya no Ba " (The Camp Scene). That point will be discussed later on.

There are naturally two different sets of costumes for Kumagai. One consists of a *kimono* of black velvet and a *kamishimo* of rich red silk fabric. The other consists of a brown silk *kimono* and a black cotton *kamishimo* which is gorgeously embroidered with gold and silver thread. The make-up is also slightly different in the two cases, though in either case, the face is painted whitish-red with a mixture of white face paint and polishing powder, over which is drawn a *kumadori*. The hero, dressed and made-up in such a way, is to make his favorite *miye* in a scene which has been dramatically reached. Kumagai, who is one of our legendary national heroes, after tasting every bitterness of war, turns into a

pacifist. The incentive that converts him into a pacifist is to be found, of course, in the battlefield of
" Suma no Ura." In the scene of " Suma no Ura,"
Kumagai uses a special wig, which is hardly ever
used by any other person. The name of this wig,
written in Chinese characters, means " lion's hide."
(By " hide " is probably meant the hide on which
the lion's mane grows : it, therefore, practically
means the lion's mane.) It is so called because the
hero's thick hair standing on end during his over-
whelming fury reminds one of a raging lion with a
bristling mane. So the *miye* at the end of the scene
of " Suma no Ura " shows how his sorrow has grown
into deep indignation. This anger, which might
be called the " eternal anger," is presented in a form
of exceeding beauty. There we see indescribable
pictorial beauty combined with a statuesque effect.
And through the great beauty created on the stage
we of the modern era, or rather of the present day,
still feel the deep anger burning in Kumagai.

Of course, the playwright might not have been
conscious of creating any such emotion when he
wrote the play. The actors might not have thought
or felt so deeply either. For, if they had written
and acted a play with such a deliberate purpose, they
would have been arrested on the spot, and might
have been crucified. Therefore, it is not likely that
they were conscious of any such intention. Never-

theless, they must surely have felt it in some way·
Otherwise, how could we explain the reason why
they chose for Kumagai in that scene the special
wig symbolical of such anger? For the keynote of
the scene of " Suma no Ura " is the anger that lies
beneath the deep sorrow, which is symbolized by
the wig Kumagai wears in that scene.   Let us con-
clude, for the moment, our discussion of the pictorial
beauty of the *Kabuki* and proceed to its musical beauty.

The music has, because of its dramatic quality,
been the most essential part of the *Kabuki*, and that
is why the *Kabuki* has often been compared with the
opera.   It is, however, more like the ordinary operetta
or the contemporary musical comedy, because of the
strong local color of its music, and because the sub-
stance of the music is really ordinary speeches and
actions, though greatly exaggerated.   A *Kabuki* performance is accompanied by music from the moment
the curtain is opened;  and it continues throughout
the play, whenever an actor enters or leaves the
stage, and during the action, until the curtain is
drawn.   The music stops only when a greater stage
effect is achieved by a break.   Some part of the
accompaniment is purely abstract, but the greater
part of it is actual description of scenes.   It is closely
related to the type of drama and the role of the
actor.

Every musical instrument peculiar to the orient

is used, and the technique is elaborate and delicate. For instance, by using drumsticks of different kinds of wood, and of varying thickness, in beating the same big drum, it is possible to differentiate the patter of rain, the sound of a shower, the peal of thunder, the sound of falling snow, the thunder of an avalanche, the roar of waves of the sea, the rippling of a river, the waves on a lake, the whistling of the wind, the raging of a mountain blast, and so forth, *ad infinitum*.

The sound of the drum, indeed, colors variously the performance of *Ichinotani Futaba Gunki*. What characterises the play, however, is the *gidayū jōruri* (song narration), as we have seen in the preceding chapter. This accompanying music sings of the thoughts and feelings of the dramatis personae and the atmosphere and emotional tone of the play, like the chorus of the Greek drama. Furthermore, it accentuates the actions of the actors, speaks the lines for them, and even carries on their dialogue in part. We have used the term musical accompaniment for convenience's sake, but it is entirely different from that of a Western drama.

Let us explain here what the *gidayū jōruri* is. The *gidayū jōruri* originally belonged to the puppet-show, which, like the *Kabuki*, is one of the two great popular dramas produced in Japan in the modern era. It is a peculiar Japanese art of singing and talking.

It started at the beginning of the sixteenth century; or, to be more accurate, it was created by popularizing the art of singing medieval war stories to the accompaniment of an instrument called *biwa,* which had been imported from China. Most of the musicians who had lived by this music had been blind men. Towards the end of the medieval era, after long years of wars, life must have been hard and insecure; but the quickening of a new age must have been felt somewhere and stimulated, if not very strongly, the will for new creation in the field of such arts.

As we have said, the first *gidayū* was created at the beginning of the sixteenth century, and although it falls far short of the high literary quality of the medieval war stories, it is still very well liked by the populace. It is the story, written in a plain style, of how Minamoto Yoshitsune, an exemplar of the Japanese warrior—who is also, as we have seen, one of the chief characters in *Ichinotani Futaba Gunki*— was loved in his youth by Lady Jōruri, who was the daughter of a wealthy man in the Eastern part of Japan. A narrator told this story, accentuating it freely by the use of a fan; and the name of the heroine came to be used as the name of the art of narrating the story. About the middle of the sixteenth century, a three-stringed musical instrument whose frame was covered with snake skin was brought to Japan from the southern part of the Asiatic Continent by way of the Ryūkyū Islands, which have become very famous in the recent Second World War. The instrument was quickly improved by the use of cats' hide instead of snake skin; and named *samisen*, it came to be widely used among our forefathers. The *jōruri* narrators began to use this instrument for accompaniment instead of using the fan for accentuation. This new art of song narration achieved remarkable development when it was combined with the art of working puppets, which had been in the hands of gipsy-like players who wandered from one thriving town to another. This combined art was the origin of the still existing Japanese puppet-show (the *Ningyō Jōruri*) which is unique in the world.

Meanwhile, the *jōruri* which had been reinforced by the advent of the *samisen* developed into many schools, like numerous fires starting from the sparks of one grass fire. It was Takemoto Gidayū who created a new school by combining all the good points of the different schools and discarding all the weaknesses. He was a farm laborer who lived in the suburbs of Osaka. His real name was Gorobei, but when he became a great musician he took the *nom de guerre* of Takemoto Gidayū. By getting Chikamatsu Monzaemon, who is called the Japanese Shakespeare, to write for him, Gidayū was able to establish his work on a firm foundation. His school came to be called *gidayū jōruri*, after his *nom de guerre*. The *Bunraku* still exists as the sole *Ningyō Jōruri* following the tradition of Gidayū.

The puppet-show developed side by side with the *Kabuki* for over a century, mutually influencing each other. The *Kabuki* manner of speaking the lines which is more like singing, and the action which is like dancing, and all the other exaggerations of presentation came from the influence of the puppet-show. We might find proof of this in the fact that the majority of the representative *Kabuki* plays were originally plays of the puppet-show. *Ichinotani Futaba Gunki* is one example. When a play of the puppet-show was appropriated to the *Kabuki* where living men acted the parts, it was natural that some change should be made. However, when a play had first been a great success in the puppet-show, the *Kabuki* performance of the same piece was inevitably influenced by the presentation in the puppet-show; otherwise, the audience would be dissatisfied. Now, a puppet cannot speak, and not being able to speak, it has to depend on movement if it wants to express a thought or feeling. It, therefore, moves a great deal, and in a highly exaggerated way. There is a form of *miye* for female puppets in which the puppet standing with its back to the audience rolls its head from one side to the other while its body is bent back like a lobster. If a living man were to attempt the same *miye*, he would break his spine. Puppeteers, however, freely make the puppets act out the form because it creates a beauty of lines, even if it is unnatural. The living actors have to imitate the action as much as possible. The elaborate movement on the stage at the head-identification scene in the " Jinya no Ba " (The Camp Scene) of the three characters—Kumagai, in the center, and his wife, Sagami, and Fuji-no-Kata—comes from the puppet-show. Thus in a play derived from a puppet-show the *gidayū jōruri* not only leads the whole performance, but its rhythm closely regulates the flow of speeches as well as actions. It is actually not merely the musical accompaniment of a play; it is rather, in the full sense of the term, a musical presentation of a play. This consummation of the musical presentation has been a decisive factor in the stylization of the *Kabuki*.

Of the beauty of the stylized performance, what appeals most strongly to the dramatic imagination is the costumes. In the *Kabuki*, as in the Italian *commedia dell'arte*, the differentiation of roles was very clear from the beginning; and the costumes were designed according to the roles. A set of costumes called the *akahime* (red princess), consisting of the brightest red dresses, the upper dress of silk gorgeously embroidered, represents an unmarried lady of the upper class. There is also a costume designed to represent poverty esthetically. It is a costume worn by a *samurai* out of job or a former dandy in reduced circumstances. A pattern of different colors is printed at the shoulders to suggest patches. The combination of compound colors, however, has resulted in a great beauty of the kind advocated by the popular Japanese painter Utamaro.

Then there is the interesting art of simply and suggestively accentuating the footsteps of a person who comes running up the *hanamichi,* by the sound of the clappers which a man sitting in the left wing strikes, though one may hesitate calling this a kind of beauty. There are still other examples of stylization, such as the use of a black curtain to represent night, and the innumerable twigs of artificial cherry-blossoms hung along the upper frame of the stage from end to end to suggest a view of cherry-blossoms in their full splendor, etc. The camp in Kumagai's " Jinya no Ba " is a stylized camp; in every scene of a camp of a general the same simple architecture, with the same high floor and with the same three steps in the middle, will be found. There is an artificial door placed at the right hand side of the stage to represent the front gate. No unnecessary decoration is added; the scenery is cut down to the minimum. Furthermore, the house is built on a much smaller scale than an ordinary house in order to make the actors appear bigger than they are, and thereby to bring out their action on the stage more vividly. When an important character comes on the stage, the afore-mentioned *kurogo* follows him like a shadow in order to thrust a small wooden stool under the actor whenever he sits down. Of course, an actor does not remain sitting for ever; he must stand up again and again. Each time the actor sits down and stands up, the *kurogo* has to put down the wooden stool and take it away, without attracting the attention of the audience. The *kurogo* moves in such a way as not to offend the eye of the audience, and the audience train themselves so that they will not be bothered by the *kurogo*. Such an understanding is necessary to appreciate rightly the stylized form of the *Kabuki*. All these devices are, after all, means of showing the actors to the greatest advantage. A *Kabuki* performance centers on the actors. The actors are the champions chosen by the common people to whom they might entrust their drama and who would embody their ideals for them. Therefore, the people fervently hope that the actors, in most of their roles, will appear big and strong and handsome.

The *kumadori* of Kumagai is applied as one means of responding to that desire. The *kumadori* is generally explained as being an exaggeration of the muscles of the face; no one knows for certain. Some say that it was originally copied from the mask of the *Noh* drama; others say it was invented by watching a morning-glory open, etc. These explanations may apply to some particular *kumadori* but the technique of the *kumadori* as a whole was no doubt imported from the Chinese drama. However that may have been, the *kumadori* of the Chinese drama does not seem to have been so complicated, whereas the *kumadori* in Japan developed into such an elaborate thing that even now there exist at least a hundred different *kumadori*—of lines of indigo, bluish-black, purple, gold, etc.

One important aspect of the stylized beauty which should not be overlooked is that of the wig. The " lion's hide " wig which Kumagai wears in the " Suma no Ura " scene is used by one other character—a revolting general who kills his lord—but no other character ever uses the same wig in any other scene. There are, indeed, many wigs which are used only for specific roles. They are of complicated classes, and if all the differences in the stylized parts were to be enumerated, one would find over 500 different kinds of wigs. This range of variety shows very well how dexterous the Japanese people are in the use of their hands.

The base of a *Kabuki* wig is a thin copper plate moulded to fit the shape of the actor's head. On the outside of this copper plate is pasted a kind of silk called *habutae*, to which the hairs are stuck very carefully one by one. The copper plate has to be made to fit the head of each actor, as all actors do not have heads of the same shape; and different wigs have to be made for the same actor according to the different roles he plays. For the wigs for some roles human hair is used, while for others animal hair is used. When an actor puts on a wig, he first binds his head with another piece of *habutae*, and puts the wig on top of it. It is no easy matter to bind the head with the *habutae*. It must not be too loose, but if it is too tight, it causes headache. When amateurs put on *Kabuki* plays they often faint for that reason. Now, putting on a wig which covers the whole head—as is the case with wigs for women's roles—is not so complicated. But putting on a man's wig which leaves the bluish shaved top of the head uncovered is much more difficult. Still another piece of *habutae* has to be placed on the part of the head which is to remain exposed, and a wig consisting of the hair at the sides and the top-knot is put on top of the cloth. Then the *habutae* has to be painted until it becomes exactly the same color as the face. An actor who shows a line between the *habutae* and the face is really no good hand at make-up.

There are different forms also in the art of make-up, which are in many cases the inherited traditions of different actors' families. For the make-up of a great hero like Kumagai, the face is painted with a mixture of face paint and polishing powder, as has been explained; black is applied to the sides of the upper part of the nose, as well as to both sides of the nostrils, in order to make the nose appear high; black is also applied to the inner end of the eye, then along the lower lid to the other end, to enlarge the eye; also the lips are enlarged at both ends. All this is done to make the face appear bigger. Of course, the natural eyebrows are buried under face paint, over which thick brave-looking eyebrows are painted with oil black.

The make-up for women's roles requires still greater care, and remarkable art and forms have been created from the early days of the *Kabuki*, which can be seen from the following anecdote. Naka-mura Tomijūrō I, who died in 1786 at the age of 68, was a great *onnagata* or *oyama* actor who created the representative *Kabuki* dance called *Dōjōji*, which is supposed to be danced by a young girl. He had danced *Dōjōji* with great success many times in his long career; and his last performance was also a great success. Now, when the old man nearing seventy announced his intention of dancing *Dōjōji* again for the last time—the dance of a beautiful young girl—his wife tried to dissuade him, saying he had better not run the risk of making himself a laughing-stock by attempting such a thing at his advanced age. At this, Tomijūrō sat in silence for a while, but then abruptly left his house. While he was gone, a beautiful girl came to see him. His wife sent the girl away, telling her he was not at home. Presently Tomijūrō returned and asked if anybody had come to see him while he was out. His wife, made slightly jealous by his eager question, replied, " Well, yes ; she certainly was a very beautiful girl." Tomijūrō smiling in profound satisfaction said, " That girl was myself. If I can still make you take me for a real young girl, don't you think it is all right for me to attempt it on the stage? " Thus filled with unshaken confidence he danced his " last " *Dōjōji*.

That story is hardly more than a legend ; it lacks objective authenticity. One should not, however, overlook the great passion with which *onnagata* actors devoted their lives to their art. The father of this Tomijūrō, who was called Yoshizawa Ayame, is a kind of patron saint of *onnagata* actors. The following is a remark he once made : " The essential thing for an *onnagata* is charm. Even an *onnagata* who is born beautiful may lose charm if he consciously endeavors to move in the right way : and if he deliberately tries to be graceful, he will be offensive. Therefore, unless you live your everyday life as a woman, you cannot become a good *onnagata*. While you are on the stage, if you should be conscious of some gesture of yours as characteristically feminine, that moment you have become very masculine. Your everyday life is most important." The key to understanding the true beauty of the *Kabuki*, indeed, will be found in realizing the fact that the stylization of the *Kabuki* has been developed and refined through such a realistic attitude on the part of the actors.

As we have said earlier, there are two forms of producing the scene of Kumagai's camp, which show the process by which the *Kabuki* technique of production has been refined while the same plays were repeated over and over again until it reached its present form. One is the newer form, the other, the older; both of them are used now. There are differences in the minute details of make-up and costumes; and although they are found only in Kumagai, it would be too complicated to compare every minute point of difference. Let us, therefore, mention one conspicuous difference. It is found in the ending of the play. In the older form of production, all the dramatis personae remain on the stage, and appear like a relief of a group of people, producing the beauty of a well-composed picture, when the curtain is drawn. In the newer form, which has been explained in the previous chapter, Kumagai alone walks down the *hanamichi*; his action still goes on after the curtain is drawn on the stage. The older form follows the tradition of the puppet-show while the newer form utilizes the *hanamichi* which is peculiar to the *Kabuki*. The two are the accepted forms of production of the camp scene of *Ichinotani Futaba Gunki*. While we are on the subject, we might also mention the fact that the present production of the scene of " Suma no Ura " is different from that of a century ago. In a play-book used before the Meiji Restoration (1868), the stage direction at the end of the scene says: " Signs of the gradual break of day in the distance. The sun is pulled out. Windows on the east and west are to be opened." These are of course directions that were followed in the days before electric lights. " Windows on the east and west " refer to the windows at the back of the second floor galleries on the east and west of the hall. These windows for letting in the light were closed during a night scene. " Signs of the gradual break of day in the distance " would mean probably that the setting was lighted up by means of candles. Now, " the sun is pulled out " must have meant that a big red painted sun was pulled out little by little from a hole in the back drop. The present-day presentation of Kumagai— the intellectual presentation, with emphasis on psychology, and with very little movement—would not harmonize with such stage effects.

The *Kabuki* is no doubt a stylized presentation; but it has not entirely escaped the waves of realism which have touched every popular drama of the modern age. If it looks stabilized now, it may only mean that it has been washed against a precipice and is floating there on a deep pool. There are many plays, however, which consummated an unchangeable form a long time before the *Kabuki* reached the precipice against which the tides of time are always washing, and they still remain the most sublimely beautiful dramatic presentations. Of all such plays the supreme piece—a grand feast of all the beauties of the *Kabuki*—is *Sukeroku Yukari no Edozakura*, one of the *Kabuki Jūhachiban*. The *Kabuki Jūhachiban* are the eighteen famous plays that are traditional in the family of Ichikawa Danjūrō, the greatest family of *Kabuki* actors. *Sukeroku Yukari no Edozakura*, or *Sukeroku* for short, is one of the best pieces among the eighteen plays. The family of Danjūrō, which has had nine Danjūrōs, still remains a great actors' family, having produced as many as five of the greatest *Kabuki* actors, Danjūrō the First, the Second, the Fourth, the Seventh, and the Ninth. A very promising young actor, who is a relative of the Danjūrō family, is now expected to succeed to the name and become Danjūrō the Tenth. (How will he fare in the storms of changing times?) *Sukeroku* has always been the great favorite of this actors' family, and has been presented again and again by succeeding generations of Danjūrōs, who have been authorities in its production. One reason, indeed, for the consummate accomplishment of the play was that it always had an authority in its production.

The scene of *Sukeroku* is the gay quarters at the time of cherry-blossoms—the pleasure resort of the people. The scene is laid in front of a *geisha* house. Sukeroku, a gallant of the *chōnin* class (the lowest of the four classes: *samurai*, farmers, artisans, tradesmen), and Ikyū, the *samurai*, quarrel over the famous *geisha* Agemaki. That is the story. Although it is a one-act play, if it were produced exactly as it used to be, it would take at least three whole hours. The quarrel is a mere quarrel over a woman, but it is made into a most elaborate play. Besides, in the quarrel the *chōnin* always gets the upper hand. Furthermore, the *geisha* Agemaki, who is the cause of this quarrel, is over head and heels in love with Sukeroku, and mercilessly makes fun of the *samurai*, telling him she could never mistake him for Sukeroku, even in the blackest of nights, for the two are as different as snow and coal. One wonders how such a play could have been produced in an age when the warrior class held absolute sway. The fact is, a convenient smoke-screen is provided to conceal the true nature of the story. That is, the true identity of Sukeroku is supposed to be Soga on Gorō (a legendary medieval warrior, who was as popular as Yoshitsune.) His brother Jūrō also appears in this play in disguise. Behind this smoke-screen the play took great liberties and provided the common people with a chance to satisfy their grudge against the ruling class. It is of great interest to see the people's resistance against the society of the time. Nowadays, however, the play is rudely cut and takes only about an hour and a half.

The outfit of Sukeroku, which is the idealized style of dress for the man of fashion of the time, has undergone, roughly speaking, three stages of changes. In the first performance of *Sukeroku* produced by Danjūrō II in March, 1713, Sukeroku wore a black *kimono* and a head-band of reddish-yellow. In the second production of the play three years later by the same Danjūrō, the head-band was of purple; and Sukeroku came on the stage holding an open paper umbrella in place of the *shakuhachi* (Japanese flute) which he had flourished in his hand as he made his appearance in the first performance. The quarrel also had become much more graceful. In the third performance, which took place twenty-nine years later, the outer garment, although still of the same black on the outside, now had a red lining, and an under-garment of pale blue was added. (Cf. Photograph) This last costume is approximately the same as that used now.

The first attraction of the play *Sukeroku* is the scene where Sukeroku, dressed in the above-mentioned dashing costume, appears on the *hanamichi* and engages in a strong masculine movement to the accompaniment of a *jōruri* piece called *Katō Bushi*, old music of very slow tempo, which seems as if it had survived solely for this one play. It is a simple unsophisticated dance which brings out the beauty of Sukeroku's costume. The performance by Danjūrō IX, who died in September, 1903, at the age of sixty-five, is still considered to have been the typical performance of *Sukeroku*.

Danjūrō IX was a very powerful actor who created the new form of presentation of Kumagai's camp scene, and whose influence is still felt in the *Kabuki* today. In fact, it was he that introduced a new mode of presentation for our *Kabuki*, placing great emphasis on the characterization of each part and on psychological delineation. He also attempted to revolutionize the performance of classic plays by insisting on making the costumes more correct historically and more logical, instead of using costumes of the modern era regardless of the actual period of the play—whether ancient or medieval. Furthermore, he had the ability for very powerful and weighty acting, and he was considered the greatest *Kabuki* actor of the modern era. Kumagai in *Ichinotani Futaba Gunki* was one of his favorite parts. In January, 1890, he produced the scene of " Suma no Ura " for the first time in Kyoto, with the part of Atsumori acted by Nakamura Ganjirō, who, after the death of

Danjūrō, became the greatest and most popular *Kabuki* actor in the Western part of Japan. Now Atsumori in this scene has to be Kojirō at the same time, though the fact is supposed to be unknown to the audience. It is, therefore, a very difficult role; and the young Ganjirō who had only just begun his successful career asked Danjūrō how he should act his part. The only answer Danjūrō gave him was that Ganjirō should simply look straight into Kumagai's eyes while he, as Atsumori, was being held under by Kumagai, when the two were supposed to look at each other. The first day came. Ganjirō, held under by Danjūrō, stared up at his big eyes. Then he saw the famous big eyes of Danjūrō slowly fill with tears. The young Ganjirō was transported at the sight. That is one of the anecdotes told about Danjūrō. It shows that Danjūrō was of the type of great actors who excel in sustained psychological presentation.

Danjūrō, furthermore, was a great orator. In the *Kabuki* there are many scenes for actors to show their oratorical power, which has a kind of musical beauty. In *Sukeroku*, there is a long speech of self-introduction delivered by Sukeroku on the stage after he has finished the dance-like movement on the *hanamichi*. Danjūrō was well suited for Sukeroku in this scene also. When Ikyū and his retainers make their appearance on the stage, they stand in a row on the *hanamichi*, facing the audience in the pit, and deliver in sonorous voices a highly poetic speech, sentence by sentence, by turns, in a tone intermediate between singing and speaking. This has a peculiar musical beauty which intoxicates the audience.

There is also another method of producing musical beauty, or of awakening a delicate dramatic emotion through the speeches. An actor A appears on the *hanamichi* and delivers a soliloquy. Another actor B simultaneously utters a soliloquy on the stage. But the stage and the *hanamichi* are supposed to be two different places—that is, a greater distance is supposed to lie between the two places than is usually understood to be the case. The soliloquys by A and B are delivered without any apparent connection, but nevertheless the actual words spoken by A and B are related with each other and form one continuous speech. The A and B in such a case are, so to speak, the obverse and reverse sides of one sad fate; both are kindly disposed towards each other, and one may be contemplating a means by which he may save the life of the other, but by some unfortunate accidental turn of events one may kill the other the very next moment.

In one play, five *otokodate* (chivalrous commoners) come on the *hanamichi* one by one, called forth by songs and musical accompaniment which reveal the character of each man. These men, like Sukeroku, sing a poetic speech of self-introduction, which is full of adjectives. Such beauty of exaggerated rendition of speeches is seen in many *Kabuki* plays, but is used in *Sukeroku* in the fullest and freest way.

In addition to the above-mentioned pictorial beauty, musical beauty, and the beauty of form, what characterizes *Sukeroku* most strongly is the great theatrical art produced by the people who created a sublime beauty out of the combined effect of the stage, the audience, and the atmosphere that envelopes the whole theatre. It has been created not by the professional actors or producers or playwrights only, but by the "people who truly love the drama," which include all such professional people, but the center is the audience. The *Kabuki* represents a free romanticism of the comman man which is in striking contrast with the newly created realism achieved by Stanislavsky in his Moscow theatre. The *Kabuki* has created a world of the purest dramatic presentation, which is not merely a play, or a picture, or a piece of music, but is indeed a flaming pillar of the most dazzling beauty, which is little less than the creation on earth of the nearest possible approach to a Paradise. For this great achievement, we may presume to say that our *Kabuki* does not fall behind the great creation of the Moscow theatre.

However that may be, having declared the dramatic value of *Sukeroku*, we should proceed to demonstrate further its unique merits as a drama. Before we do so, however, we must explain to our readers, or our audience, the general construction of the original *Kabuki* theatre. The *Kabuki* theatre where you saw *Ichinotani Futaba Gunki* was not the real *Kabuki* theatre. A new form of presentation may or may not develop out of that theatre in the future, but that is irrelevant to our subject at present. The theatre with the very flat but wide stage must have struck you as a very odd construction. This queer theatre is nothing but a hobgoblin of the calculating machine, created by the present commercialism.

The former theatre where the classical plays called the *Kabuki* plays were performed was only about one-fifth the size of the present *Kabuki* theatre. And the width of the stage was less than half that of the present stage. The reason why the upper frame of the stage was low even for the small theatre was that the Tokugawa government restricted the height of the beams of a theatre from the standpoint of fire-prevention. The basic esthetic plan of the *Kabuki* was to make the actors appear as big as possible, and as near to the audience as possible, on such a small stage, compared with that of the present. And parallel with the present *hanamichi*, there used to be a second *hanamichi* which was about half the width of the other. These two *hanamichi* were connected with each other, at a point about three fourths the length of the hall from the stage, by a passage separating the first and second class seats. An actor was able, therefore, to walk around the audience while acting.

Now, for the performance of *Sukeroku*, the setting of the main stage was the front of a *geisha* house. The entrance was on the left hand side, and facing it was a lattice-work of brownish-red, behind which hung a green bamboo-blind. Behind the blind sat the *tayū* and *samisen* players of the *Katō Bushi* to which Sukeroku was to dance. The musicians in former days were not professionals; they were all amateurs. They were bosses of the fish market who were patrons of the *Kabuki*. They were there at their own expense in order to help the performance of *Sukeroku*. To the right was a street lamp, under which was placed a water-tub. This was to be used later by Sukeroku to hide himself from the pursuing mob. It was really filled with water, so that when Sukeroku plunged into it, the water flowed over onto the stage. It is said that when Danjūrō VIII performed Sukeroku, the water of the tub was afterwards sold for so much a cupful. The reason probably was that he was then a brilliant rising star of the *Kabuki*, but the story also shows how great the people's excitement was over a great *Kabuki* performance. The water of the tub sold in that way is said to have been used by young girls to dilute their face paint.

To return to the stage of *Sukeroku*. There were twigs of cherry-blossoms hanging from the ceiling. The scenery would have helped one to realize the beauty referred to by our great modern poet of the people in his *haiku* (poems of five, seven, and five syllables) :

> Clouds of cherry-blossoms ;
> Whence the sound of that temple bell
> —From Uyeno or from Asakusa?

Sukeroku, after killing Ikyū, hid himself in the water-tub, having lost every means of escape. This dandy, who is comparable to Cyrano de Bergerac in his witty sarcasm, was surrounded by the hue and cry of the pursuing mob which was heard from behind the curtains on both sides of the stage and at the ends of both *hanamichi*. Just then the temple bell began to ring. This remarkable presentation, making full use of the moment of relaxation between the climax and the end of the scene, seems to symbolize the full beauty of the whole performance.

Let us return once again to the setting. Along the balustrades of the galleries on either side of the first and second floors were hung flowered *noren* (shop-curtains or screens), crimson rugs, and green bamboo-screens, to match the setting on the stage ; and a gate was placed in front of the curtain at the rear end of the *hon hanamichi* (main *hanamichi*) to represent the entrance to the gay quarters. This would imply that the seats of the audience were supposed to be placed in the flowering thoroughfare of the pleasure resort.

Before the great Earthquake of the Kantō District in 1923, *shibaijaya* (tea-houses attached to a theatre) used to stand in rows outside the theatre. These tea-houses served as information offices for the audience, as resting-places for intervals, and salons for regular *Kabuki*-goers. Although such consumption facilities had gradually decreased in number after the turn of the century, in the period when they had flourished there were over fifty or sixty houses in each of the three classes they were divided into according to their grades; the best, the medium, the inferior. The best tea-houses had the very best cooks of the day to be found in the whole city. These tea-houses were all decorated with the same decorations used for tea-houses in the gay quarters—green bamboo-screens, flowered *noren*, crimson rugs, and flowered lanterns. In front of the theatre were planted cherry-trees, and hand-lanterns were arranged in rows, just as they were in the thoroughfare of the gay quarters. Thus the setting for the gay quarters on the main stage not only enveloped the seats of the audience, but spread even to the outer block of the theatre.

*Sukeroku* was performed in just such an elaborate setting. In the play, dealing as it does with the quarrel between a *samurai* and a *chōnin* over a woman, a mob of people have to appear. *Sukeroku* is indeed a play of a mob. And the way the mob is utilized —the way they come on the stage, and the way they move there—reveals the great wisdom of the people, showing all over the play, like diamonds set in an emperor's crown. In no other *Kabuki* play do we find such a great number of people on the stage as in *Sukeroku;* neither do they play such an important part in the performance as they do in *Sukeroku.*

*Sukeroku* came to have an authentic text about the middle of the eighteenth century, when Sakurada Jisuke I, a playwright possessing a rich vocabulary, revised it and wrote it down. As he lived in the precincts of Asakusa Kanzeon, and as he is said to have been unable to sleep well unless before going to bed he took a stroll in Yoshiwara, which is the scene of *Sukeroku*, he must have known well the mob that appear in the play and must have loved them.

According to a play-book used for the performance of *Sukeroku* at Nakamuraza Theatre in March, 1774, when the curtain is opened four men are seen seated on a bench which is covered with a crimson rug, and merry-making men, including *samurai* and *chōnin*, young men of tea-houses who are carrying lighted lanterns, egg-vendors, *sushi*-sellers, massagists, etc. pass by. These people are necessary to represent the gay quarters which were the earthly Paradise of the people of the Tokugawa era. Besides, the mob in the later scene would not come alive if these people did not appear on the stage at the beginning. In the performance of the present day, however, this part is entirely cut. The producers do not realize that the brilliance of *Sukeroku* is in the use of the mob.

There are few other plays in which so many vendors appear as in *Sukeroku;* and each one of them is presented with great care. First of all there is the wine-seller, who, as has been explained, is supposed to be Soga no Jūrō Sukenari, the brother of Sukeroku. Next there comes a medicine-vendor. This man sells a kind of tonic, which, he says, has been brought from China and which we may suppose to have been something like the contemporary vitamin pills. The medicine-vendor comes on the stage to advertise his medicine. He is called the *uirō-uri*, which was originally a role in one of the *Kabuki Jūhachiban,* and which provided a chance for actors to show their oratorical power. This role was put into *Sukeroku* merely as an additional adornment. Thirdly, there comes the delivery boy of a noodle-shop. This character possesses a full portion of the pride of an Edo citizen, although he is a mere porter of a small restaurant; and in spite of his general meagre appearance he wears a wide loin-cloth of crimson silk crepe. When he is challenged into a quarrel, he blusters out at his enemy, flaunting this crimson loin-cloth. He is indeed a lovable character who might be called upon to represent the people if occasion demanded. The retainers of Ikyū, who are also part of the mob, are important characters in *Sukeroku*. It is they who start the big quarrel against the noodle-deliverer. The wine-vendor is also a role for actors to display their oratorical ability; but such speeches are omitted in most performances now, and in most performances the medicine-vendor does not appear at all.

We do not, however, mean to say that the present-day performance of the play is a complete failure. In the present-day performance in which the many passersby at the beginning of the play are omitted, the first people that appear on the stage are two night-watchmen, who come out onto the *hanamichi* from the rear. These night-watchmen are dressed in dark blue—dark blue cotton *shirushi-banten* (livery coat), *haragake* (workman's waistcoat, with no back), and *momohiki* (close-fitting trousers); they cross each other on the main stage and go in through the other *hanamichi*. After they have disappeared behind the curtain at the rear end, the sound of an iron-rod being struck on the ground is heard. There is no one on the stage then. The pantomime suggests that perfect peace and order reign in the gay quarters. Threading through, as it were, this hushed suspense, the managing actor comes out on the stage in great dignity, and, turning to the bamboo-screen on the left of the stage, says: "Musicians of the *Katō Bushi*, please begin!" His back is turned to the audience as he makes this speech, but it is not considered impolite to the audience. No other scene would represent so fully how the people's drama blessed and felicitated the peace and prosperity of the land.

The mob pours out onto the stage when the quarrel breaks out between the noodle-deliverer and Ikyū's retainers. As they are composed of all the people behind the stage, their costumes are haphazard and diverse. They are like people who might have rushed out of the kitchens of our own homes. Mingling among the mob, there comes the wine-seller, who remains crouched about the middle of the *hanamichi* after Sukeroku has driven away the mob. This method of bringing in the wine-seller is of great interest. Then the wine-seller and Sukeroku together try to provoke passersby to a quarrel. The country *samurai* and men of fashion, with whom the two try to pick a quarrel, are also a part of the mob. Towards the end of the play, when Sukeroku comes out dripping wet from the water-tub, and Agemaki helps him, the mob appear once again and discover them. There Agemaki facing the mob, delivers her famous grand splurge: "If one tip of those sticks you stupidly flourish were to touch my body, the whole town of Gochōmachi would be turned into darkness!" This is a scene in which the Paradise on earth is to turn into Hell. Whether the scene will be successfully idealized and beautified in its presentation depends partly upon the volume of the actor who plays the part of Agemaki, and partly upon the spirit of the mob and the success or failure in organizing them.

*Sukeroku* is a consummation of the pictorial beauty, the musical beauty, and the beauty of form of the *Kabuki*. And it is of interest to note that the mass of people, in their natural state, should play an important part in such a performance. It shows that the essence of the *Kabuki* lay not in any aristocratic formality, but in the very common everyday life of the people, though it was refined through the artistic sensibility of Hiroshige and Utamaro.

# Chapter III
## Kabuki Plays

*Kabuki* plays may be said to have come into existence when curtains came to be used on the stage. In the beginning, the *Kabuki* adopted the stage of the *Noh* drama, and used it without making any change. The main stage was approximately 18 feet square, to which was attached a bridge which corresponded to the *hanamichi* of the later *Kabuki* stage. The *Kabuki* plays that were performed there were all independent one-act plays, like those of the *Noh* drama. Gradually growing dissatisfied with one-act plays, theatre people invented the curtain, which enabled them to put on plays of more than one act. That event took place in 1664. It was about this time also that the curtain came to be used on the Italian stage, so the history of the *Kabuki* parallels the development of Western drama. When the curtain came to be used, it was necessary to consider the connection between one act and the next, and also the right place to close an act. This necessity stimulated the growth and development of the art of dramatic composition.

It is impossible to tell how much literary value

the first full length play had, for there is no extant copy of the play. According to records of the time, the first long play presented in Osaka was *Hinin no Adauchi* (Revenge of the Outcast), written by Fukui Yagozaemon, while the first one to be performed in Edo (the name of Tokyo until 1868) was *Imagawa Shinobi Guruma* (the Rout at Imagawa) by Miyako Dennai. Both Fukui Yagozaemon and Miyako Dennai resembled Shakespeare and Molière in that they were actors as well as playwrights. In the early periods of the development of drama in every country the playwrights were actors. Tominaga Heibei, the first playwright to have his name and title written on the program, was also an actor as well.

The first professional playwright, however, came into existence fairly early in the history of the *Kabuki*. This was Chikamatsu Monzaemon, who is called the Shakespeare of Japan. It is on record that he died at the age of seventy-two in 1724; he must, therefore, have been born in 1653. Not much is known of his life or career, as is the case with Shakespeare. But it is known for a fact that he was born into a family of *samurai*, and that he had a fairly good upbringing. At first he served as a retainer in a nobleman's house, but later he became a playwright, which meant, as far as social standing was concerned, lowering himself to the very bottom stratum of society. He began by writing *Kabuki* plays for Sakata Tōjurō.

Later he came to write puppet-show plays for Take-moto Gidayū the First, and Takemoto Gidayū the Second. There is no material ground to explain why he gave up writing *Kabuki* plays and began to write for the puppet-show; but it is generally surmised that he found little attraction in the *Kabuki* after Tōjurō quit the stage. Tōjurō died in 1709 at the age of sixty-three, but the last few years before his death, he had suffered from ill-health and was obliged to give up his postition as *zamoto* (the proprietor) of the Miyako Mandayū Troupe of Kyoto, for which he had worked very hard for many years. It was about that time that Chikamatsu wrote his first domestic *jōruri* play, *Sonezaki Shinjū* (Sonezaki Double Suicide), for Gidayū the First. Chikamatsu had in fact written both *jōruri* and *Kabuki* plays from the very beginning of his period of training. *Genji Kuyō* (A Mass for the *Genji Monogatari*), which is supposed to have been written by him when he was twenty-four, is a *jōruri*, while *Fujitsubo no Onryō* (The Ghost of Fujitsubo), which brought him sudden fame, was written the very next year, for the Miyako Mandayū Troupe. The text of the *Kabuki* play, however, survives only in the form of an *eiri kyōgen bon* (an illustrated text), which gives merely the rough out-line of the play. His full scope as a playwright, therefore, has to be made out of his puppet-show plays. There are eighty historical plays and twenty-four domestic or social dramas extant, the latter representing his most mature philosophy of life and technique of playwriting. These plays depict fully and vividly the life of men and women struggling to live true to human nature within the severe laws and restrictions of a feudal world. It was an age when the humanity of the people awakened in the medieval age was still alive with a desire for freedom of passion, which was to be checked by feudalistic morals until it was extinguished. Until the very last moment before its extinction, people relished the joy of life and the beauty of nature. Such feelings are vividly expressed in the passages of the *michiyuki* (elopement scene) of *Sonezaki Shinjū*.

" Farewell to life; farewell to night! As we walk to death, our lives are like the frost on the road through Adashi-gahara, which is crushed and gone at every step we take ; a dream of a dream, so vain, so transient. The seven morning bells. Hark! The sixth has rung, leaving one more—the last bell we shall hear on earth. It tells of that peace and joy attained by transcending both life and death. It is not only the bell that we are leaving for ever, but the grass, and the trees, and the sky—in the sky as we look up in parting there floats an indifferent cloud. The cool rippling of the water of the river ! How coldly shines the North Star, reflected on the river, and the milky way—the stars of man and wife. This bridge of Umeda will be for us a bridge of magpies' wings. Magpies spread their wings in a row across the milky way to let Altair meet Vega on the night of the seventh of July. Crossing this bridge, we shall remain for ever man and wife. Nothing shall part us as we thus firmly embrace each other at the last; and the tears we shed will cause the water of the river to rise."

Chikamatsu's philosophy of art is represented by his following words: "Art is the layer that lies between the skins of truth and falsity . . . That which is false but not false, true but not true—that is what gives joy." From his long years of experiences as a playwright, he had come to that conclusion concerning the world of fiction which a playwright should create. The *Kabuki* towards the end of the seventeenth century and through the beginning of the eighteenth century, represented by Chikamatsu and Tōjurō, evidently had a new perception and a theory suitable for a new era. They are clearly seen in the two valuable books, *Nijinshū* and *Kengaishū*, in which Tōjurō's theory of dramatic presentation is expounded. These people were in favor of realistic presentation, emphasizing speeches, following in the tradition of the *Noh* drama of the middle age. If that tendency had naturally and freely developed, the *Kabuki* might perhaps have run in a track similar to that of the Western drama. One indirect reason why it did not develop that way was the isolation policy adopted by the Tokugawa Shogunate government, the policy of wilfully closing the nation's doors against the world where endless roads of transportation were being developed over the seas. As for direct reasons, the first was the isolation of the *Kabuki* from the intellectual classes; the second was the tradition among the laboring classes of spending all they earned each day, and not saving any money for the future; the third was the inevitable tendency to over-emphasize form.

For about thirty years after the death of Chikamatsu, the puppet-show continued to flourish, overpowering the *Kabuki*. Yoshida Bunzaburō, a great puppet-show man, made his puppets act exactly as if they were living human beings. The technique for three men to manipulate one puppet was also invented during this period. It may well have been that human beings, whose freedom of action was severely restricted, entrusted the puppets with their unattainable dreams. Also, a new method of having more than one playwright collaborate in writing a play was inaugurated among the group of playwrights after they had lost their great master Chikamatsu.

In this system of collaboration, the first playwright would choose a subject and work out the outline of the whole story, or all the collaborators would meet and decide on it. After that, the first playwright, the second, the third, the fourth, etc. would write that part of the play which had been assigned to him and thus together make up a play. When this system was adopted, each playwright naturally poured all his strength into his allotted portion; and the result was that each part took on a quality of independence. Another method was for a number of playwrights, say three, to choose a theme, say the parting of parent and child, and to vie with one another in working out a new composition and new devices. Those practices are the reasons why many of the classical *Kabuki* plays are extant today in the form of one-act plays, and why there are many plays with similar compositions. Both *Ichinotani Futaba Gunki* and *Sukeroku Yukari no Edozakura*, discussed in previous chapters, were originally part of lengthy many act plays which took a whole day to perform.

Now, the puppet-show which had enjoyed great popularity for years passed its peak of prosperity around 1748, after which it gradually showed signs of decline, until in about twenty years it came down to a complete slump. On the other hand great figures appeared among *Kabuki* playwrights. Namiki Shōzō who invented the revolving stage in 1758, was a pupil of the puppet-show writer Namiki Sōsuke, who was, incidentally, the first writer of *Ichinotani Futaba Gunki*. Among the pupils of Shōzō were two outstanding playwrights; Namiki Gohei, and Nagawa Kamesuke. Gohei wrote the famous domestic play *Godairiki Koi no Fūjime* (Godairiki Seal of Love). In 1778 he left his native place Osaka and went to Edo, where he settled for the rest of his life. This shows that the centre of the *Kabuki* had moved from the Keihan district (district around Osaka and Kyoto) to Edo. In Edo at the time lived Sakurada Jisuke the

First, who was some years Gohei's senior. Also a new playwright named Tsuruya Nanboku IV (the first three Tsuruya Nanbokus had been actors; the fourth, who had been adopted into the family, became a playwright) appeared, after whom came Kawatake Mokuami, who is considered to have been the great consummator of the *Kabuki*. Jisuke was a dandy; Gohei was the son of a proprietor of a tea-house attached to a theatre; Nanboku was the son of a dyer's pattern printer; Mokuami was the junior master of a pawn-shop: they all belonged to the people. Naturally they were not very good at writing historical plays depicting men in armor or *kamishimo* (ceremonial dress); their best works are all domestic plays. There are only a few plays, however, that have really interesting dialogue. *Sukeroku Yukari no Edozakura*, whose definitive text is supposed to have been written by Jisuke, is one of the few.

There is a scene in *Sukeroku* where Sukeroku interferes with Monbei, a henchman of Ikyū, when he is quarrelling with the noodle-vendor.

Monbei: Hey! You cur. Stop.

Noodle-vendor: Please sir; pardon me, sir.

Monbei: What's that? "Pardon me?" You hit a man with your noodle-box and say, "Pardon me"? You noodle-dog, you bean-paste cur, you used-tea-leaves slave! Couldn't you see me? You, you—

(He pushes the noodle-vendor and strikes him.)

Noodle-vendor: Please forgive me, sir. Please, courtesans,

— 71 —

please apologize for me.

All: Monbei-san, forgive him. Do.

Monbei: I won't. No, I won't.

All: Sukeroku-san, apologize for him. Apologize for him, please. . . .

(All beg Sukeroku to interfere. Sukeroku twists back Monbei's arm.)

Monbei: Ow, ouch! You hurt!

Sukeroku: All right. You get out; quick.

Noodle-vendor: Thanks, sir.

(He starts towards the *hanamichi*.)

Monbei: Stop! Stop, I say.

Sukeroku: That's all right. You fool. Why don't you hurry away?

(The noodle-vendor starts to leave again.)

Monbei: I'll strike you to death if you move.

Sukeroku: It's all right, I say. It's time you forgave the fellow.

Monbei: Time I forgave the fellow?

Sukeroku: Exactly. Let him go.

Monbei: What's that? Let him go? I don't want to let him go. What then? What if I won't?

Sukeroku: Look here, man. Don't act childish. Let him go.

Monbei: You've been quite offensive. Don't you know who I am?

Sukeroku: Why, certainly. Everyone knows you. You are known not only here in Yoshiwara, but everywhere— all over Edo.

Monbei: You know me, you say?

Sukeroku: I don't know you at all.

This kind of dialogue, through which is revealed the life of the people in the background, is found in episodic parts of a play which are more or less unrelated to the main story. It shows that the technique was fixed before the play was composed. By the latter half of the eighteenth century, many rules and forms were established in the *Kabuki*, and they restricted free creation. There were stiff restrictions particularly for playwrights.

A *Kabuki* play was never provided by people outside the theatre. A play was written by the playwrights attached to a theatre or troupe to suit the actors of that troupe. A *sakusha-beya* (playwrights' room) consisted of playwrights numbering from three or four up to as many as twelve or thirteen. The playwrights took the place of stage-managers in a broad sense; that is, they had to attend to everything connected with the production of a play: reading the play, *kakinuki* (copying the part of each actor), allocation of parts, direction of rehearsals, ordering of stage property, costumes, and musical instruments, signalling the opening and closing of the curtain, *kōken* (prompting), and advertisements during a performance, etc. A playwright, therefore, not only attended to literary creation but trained himself as a producer through years of experience behind the stage, and his art and technique were handed down to his pupils. In *Kozairoku,* written by Gohei the Second, which is practically the only extant book of the time on the art of dramatic composition, we find the following passage :

" The drama is a castle, the *zamoto* (owner of the theatre), is the general, the actors are the warriors, and the playwright is the commander. If the commander were not high-spirited, the warriors would not obey his orders; and the orderly battle array of the play being thrown into confusion, it would not be able to conquer its foe, the audience, but would be routed like undisciplined soldiers, and be buried in the moat."

That shows the spirit of the playwright. Although the statement shows that the playwrights had a sense of pride in their position, actually they were overpowered by the tendency to value actors above everything, and were not able to give free course to their creative power. One generation before Jisuke the First, there lived a playwright named Kanai Sanshō, who always kept a long sword by his side when he read his play to the actors. It is said that he looked as if he were ready to kill any actor who might make any objections to the play. Jisuke on his death bed is reported to have said in bitter lamentation, " When I am dead, do not offer prayers for my soul, but be sure to keep the Edo plays thriving. In thirty years, plays will come to be written by actors, as is now the case in the Keihan district." Thus the plays of the *Kabuki* had to be written with special consideration for the characteristics and inclinations of the actors of each troupe. Besides, there were many specific forms to be observed. For instance, the New Year Performance of the *Kabuki* in Edo had to have for its theme the Soga Brothers—their act of revenge on the murderer of their father. New devises had to be created within that restriction. As a result, there would be created a play in which, for instance, Soga no Gorō would be Sukeroku.

The actors were allotted to the three *Kabuki* theatres in Edo each year. The first performance after the allocation was called the *kaomise* (face showing) performance, which always took place in November. And in the *kaomise* program, the one-act play *Shibaraku* (Wait a Moment) was always included. *Shibaraku*, like *Sukeroku*, is one of the *Kabuki Jūhachiban*. It was the favorite play of generations of the Ichikawa Danjūrō family, and that was why it became a rule to include it in the *kaomise*. Furthermore, in a day's program, at least one or two acts had to be dance-scenes.

*Sewamono* were the social dramas of the day, and one would expect them to be freer in form. As a matter of fact, however, there was the rule of the *miseba* (the important scenes to attract the audience) and it was required of the playwright to include all the necessary *miseba* in every play, because they made it easier for the playwright to write the play, actors to act the play, and the audience to understand it. Gradually this practise of creating the *miseba* developed into a hard and fast absolute rule. Among the *miseba* there are the *nureba*, the *koroshiba*, the *semeba*, the *yusuriba*, the *sewaba*, etc.

The *nureba* is not a mere love scene. The purpose of the *nureba* is to create a scene of extreme obscenity, as daring as the horror of the *koroshiba*. In the old copies of texts, we come across many passages that do not bear reading now. Such passages are found, however, mostly in parting words and stage directions, and therefore may be cut without affecting very much the main story of the play. If a woman were acting a woman's part, it would be very simple to create strong sex appeal—all she would have to do would be to remove one by one the veils which enfold her until she would be naked. In the *Kabuki*, however where men act women's parts, it is not so simple. Great art is required in the suggestive actions for stimulating the imagination of the audience.

A *koroshiba* is a bloody scene, whose purpose is to create horror. Merely killing ten men at once, or even a hundred men, does not constitute a *koroshiba*. In a *koroshiba* the victim is killed by slow bloody torture. As the purpose of the *koroshiba* is to make the audience shudder in horror, it is usually accompanied by a ghost story. The ghost of the victim appears to torment the killers; and the audience is doubly horrified.

A *semeba* is usually a scene of torture. In the old days there was a method of torture called *kotozeme*, which was a mental torture in which the victim was made to play the *koto* or *samisen* or *kokyū* in order that the torturers might know his true thoughts and feelings. But the *semeba* in the *Kabuki* play is no such mild affair. As in the *koroshiba*, the purpose of the scene is to create horror. Methods called the *yukizeme* (torture with snow), and the *hebizeme* (torture by snakes), etc. are used; but the artificial snow and artificial snakes do not create as powerful an effect of horror as that of a *koroshiba*. The best that could be expected was to let a rising star actor take the part of the victim and make his fans hold their breaths. In most *semeba* the victim of torture is a powerless beautiful young lady, and the result is a scene of fantasm.

Thus the *koroshiba* and the *nureba*, if not the *semeba*, sometimes are too bold and have to be toned down. On the other hand a *yusuriba* is most frequently used in various forms, and is an indispensable *miseba* of a *sewamono*. It is a scene in which the victim is robbed of his money by a blackmailer who finds one pretext after another for demanding the money. As this scene is close to the actual daily life of the people, it easily appeals to the audience. For the actors, it is a convenient device for displaying their power of realistic presentation. Since it is a *miseba*, both the blackmailer and the blackmailed are played by representative actors. But when two great actors are in opposition, it will not do for one to win and the other to be completely overpowered; moreover, the actor who has to take the losing man's part will not consent. Therefore, it is necessary for the scene to end n a draw, and that is where the playwright has to apply all his resources.

Now, a *sewaba* is less difficult and more effective than a *yusuriba*. It is a scene which depicts the most helpless financial difficulty. Even a rich family may occasionally be hard pressed for money, but such a difficulty does not constitute an effective scene. The poverty depicted in a *sewaba* is absolute destitution, in which the dramatis personae involved struggle and struggle with no hope of ever obtaining the money they desperately need. Children are always used in a *sewaba*. It is the most conventional method, and it has been criticized by some people who think it is not fair to use children for an effect on the stage. Besides the children, there is in many cases an invalid who adds to the difficulty. Then there comes a creditor to demand payment of his money. In addition to all such sad conditions, the hero feels it his duty to save his master, to whom he owes a debt of gratitude and who is now, like himself, in grave financial difficulty, or his son who has been apprenticed to some master is robbed of his master's money while he was out on an errand; or his daughter whom he has just sold to a brothel is found to have eloped with her lover, and so on. Afflictions pour upon the protagonists one on top of another and the hero goes through a bitter lamentation saying: " Of all the hundreds of evils on earth, there is nothing so cruel as poverty."

As a *sewaba* had to seem real for its effect, one would expect it to depend solely on a realistic presentation. However, as a matter of fact, both playwright and actor endeavoured to bring in musical effects. That was especially a marked tendency after the middle of the eighteenth century when plays of the puppet-show began to be given on the *Kabuki* stage. For instance, in a *sewaba*, *gidayū* accompaniment was always used. That would make it necessary for the speeches and the actions to harmonize with the music, and would mean a restriction on realistic actions. But it was welcomed as a means of creating dramatic sentiment and fantasy. It meant a weakening of the spirit of realism that had been strong in the *Kabuki* in the Genroku era, and it meant also a strengthening of the tendency towards stylization and formalism of the *Kabuki* as an amusement and an entertainment for festivals.

In a *sewamono* there is always a pantomime scene called *sewa danmari*. There used to be a custom of presenting a pantomime to introduce the new members of a troupe at the *kaomise* performance. That was the orthodox pantomime, and it was inserted in a historical play. This form was adopted into the *sewamono* and became *sewa danmari*. A *danmari* originally was a

— 79 —

pantomime showing a number of people meeting by
accident on a dark night in front of a small shrine in
a valley, or some such place. In a *sewamono* the scene
may be laid at a seashore on a dark night, or on the
bank of a river, where the main characters appear.
As it is a place where people naturally pass by, it does
not seem strange for the main characters to cross each
other there. Therefore, a *sewa danmari* is a very convenient scene for the playwrights. They adopt the
peculiar form of the orthodox pantomime to a freer
and more realistic use in the *sewamono*.

The *nagauta* which came to be used for *Kabuki*
accompaniment achieved rapid growth and development in the beginning of the nineteenth century,
when the musical production of the *Kabuki* came to
be the peculiar form embracing the whole *Kabuki*
drama. For instance, in the speeches of a *yusuriba*
a special oratorical art called *yakuharai* is used. It is
so called because it reminds one of the street entertainment of *yakuharai* on the eve of Risshun (the first
day of spring). An ordinary dialogue is carried on
until it comes to the important lines, when the speeches
are suddenly turned into sonorous chanting. When
that part is over, the ordinary tone of dialogue is
resumed. It is a very queer technique, when one
comes to think of it; but one reason for it is that it
was necessary to devise a means which would enable
the audience to catch every word of the important

speeches. The theatres of those days were crude wooden buildings, after they had been burned down and rebuilt many times; and as there was hardly any acoustics in those theatres, the lines did not carry well. It was necessary, therefore, for the speakers to raise their voices a few degrees above that of the ordinary dialogue when they came to important passages. Another factor which promoted the development of the musical performance of the *Kabuki* was the natural inherent essence of the *Kabuki* which had developed under the influence of the *Noh* drama. Such a tendency in the *Kabuki* took advantage of the marked general weakening of the realistic spirit in the *Kabuki* at the time. Having thus lost its free creative power, the *Kabuki* developed into sensual formalism, and all efforts were concentrated on refining its art and technique.

Towards the middle of the nineteenth century, the complacent isolationism of Japan was gradually undermined. Noises of the modern world, of England and other European nations, began to disturb the happy dream of the Japanese people. The *Kabuki*, too, could not, by instinct, completely shut out the fresh if somewhat restless sounds, like the chirping of birds on a May morning, though it frowned in bewilderment. The first effect was seen in the change in the historical plays. A *Kabuki* program had consisted of one lengthy play which included historical acts and *sewamono*, and which started in the morning and lasted until evening. Gohei at one time insisted that there should be two independent plays, the first a historical play, and the second a *sewamono*; but the custom of putting on one long play that took a whole day to perform continued until the end of the Tokugawa era. That form seems to have started at the time of Chikamatsu. The *Kabuki* plays by Chikamatsu consist of three acts: the first more or less formal act deals with a trouble in a *daimyō* family up to the climax of the trouble, the second scene is laid in a gay quarter, where the young lord is seen disguised as a tradesman—this scene would include a love scene—the third is a dance act at a festival of a shrine or temple, where all the people connected with the incident gather and dance together to celebrate the happy solution of the trouble. The use of festivals of shrines and temples in the play reflects the strong religious temperament of the people of his age. The reason why the historical act continued for a long time to occupy the main part of a program and did not easily give way to *sewamono* was that the theatre was always a place for escape from reality. In addition to that, the people of the time were not very strongly social conscious; besides, it was difficult to bring in actual life and events of the day because of the severe restrictions placed by the government. The subjects of the historical plays were, therefore, taken mostly out of the middle age.

Of course, in some cases, contemporary events were represented, disguised as events of the middle age. For instance, the famous lynching by the Akō *rōshi* in 1702 was made into *Kanadehon Chūshingura* 46 years after the event, and achieved unparalleled popularity, though immediately afterwards the government strictly forbade the use of the event as a subject of a play. In the play, the act of revenge is supposed to have taken place in the Muromachi era of the middle age.

It was perhaps because of such restrictions on the choice of subjects that there was established within the theatre itself restrictions on the subject matters of historical plays. They were to be the *Yorimitsu mono*, *Soga mono*, *Dōjōji mono*, *Asama mono*, etc. Yorimitsu and Soga brothers were legendary heroes, *Dōjōji* was a representative *Noh* drama, and *Asama* was a popular drama in the early history of the *Kabuki*. The playwrights one after another wrote plays on such well-known figures and events. All they were expected to do was to create a new device for treating the same subject. One would then expect them to study the history of these people and events and try to discover new facts. They did no such thing. They would have thought it showed nothing but lack of creative power on the part of the playwright if he tried to do such a thing. A proof of it might be found in *Kanadehon Chushingura*. The source of this play is of course the historical fact of the Akō *rōshi* avenging the death of their lord; but only 2 per cent of the play presents the historical fact while 98 per cent of the play is the production of the playwright's imagination. The interest of the audience is centered upon seeing what new world of fiction the playwright will create out of the conventional people and events.

The playwrights, however, were not allowed complete freedom in creating their world of imagination. For, in the historical play, as well as in the *sewamono* of the decadent period, there were the conventions of the *miseba*, such as: the *migawari*, the *harakiri*, the *monogatari*, the *michiyuki*, the *miarawashi*, etc. To explain them briefly: a *migawari* is a scene in which a person sacrifices his dearest object—his own child—for the sake of his young lord; the *harakiri* is suicide committed in order to serve one's lord. Both scenes aim at stimulating intense dismal emotions. The *monogatari* is a scene in which an important story of the past is related in such a way as to display the actor's oratorical power, as in " Kumagai Jinya." The *michiyuki* is a wayside scene where a lover and his sweetheart, driven by a villain, are seen in flight. The *miarawashi* is a scene where the ringleader of a conspiracy is exposed and a family trouble is settled. The proper arrangement of these *miseba* was a serious matter with the playwrights of historical plays, though perhaps in a slightly less degree than those of a *sewamono*.

The first actor who endeavored to fight against the restrictive formalism of the historical play was the great Danjūrō the Ninth. His idea was supported by the new reform movement of the drama which started about 1877. This was a movement supported by statesmen and scholars who had been abroad and had come in contact with Western ways. Judging from the standpoint of the essence of drama, these people must be condemned as shallow and superficial, but they had in their background the great social reformation of the time. Such a condition gave birth to a new group of historical plays called the *katsureki*. *Katsureki* was a mocking newly-coined word meaning " living history." These plays were not based on correct historical facts, but were written by dramatizing old stories in literature, such as *Taiheiki*, and *Gikeiki*. What surprised the audience most was the realistic costumes and stage setting.

The first playwright to write these new plays was, of course, Kawatake Mokuami, for there were no other playwrights besides those attached to theatres. Mokuami had to respond to the demands of the intellectual people who were the important new element in the *Kabuki* audience; he also felt it his duty to satisfy the young *zagashira*, Danjūrō. Mokuami, who had long worked with the art of the well-made play, often had to discard all his invaluable experiences as a playwright in order to create an uninteresting and unformed play of the " living history." It must have been an unsatisfying and unrequited labor for him. There is an interesting photograph of him at the age of sixty-three in a frock-coat. His face is that of a man of wisdom and culture, and though there is something of the artisan in his expression, his face would well stand comparison with that of Ibsen in his old age. In 1878, the new building of Shintomiza (the theatre which took the place of Moritaza, one of the three licensed theatres in Edo)—which had been burned down some years ago—was completed, and a grand opening ceremony was held, to which over a thousand notables in and out of official circles of the time were invited. It was, of course, a most ambitious enterprise unparalleled in the preceding history of the *Kabuki*. And the frock-coat in the picture was the one Mokuami had ordered for that one single occasion. One can imagine with what a wry face he put on that coat. The new reform movement of the drama was just like attempting to put a frock-coat all at once on the unprepared *Kabuki* which had been the friend of the populace during the long three hundred years of Japan's isolation from the world. Out of that movement, strongly political in its color, was born the present *Kabukiza*, the representative *Kabuki* theatre in Tokyo now, which was built in 1889. In this new theatre, the position of the playwright was occupied by a man who had been one of the intellectuals among the new audience of the *Kabuki*. This event was to prophesy that the system of having playwrights attached to theatres was to break down, and that playwrights of the new age were to be born outside the theatre. Historians of Japanese drama naturally consider Mokuami to be the last of the traditional *Kabuki* playwrights.

The *katsureki*, or new historical drama, was too superficial, and soon defeated itself by going too far. The rationalization of the *Kabuki* achieved during the short interval of the *katsureki* period, however, has had a decisive influence on the *Kabuki* over half a century. The powerfulness of the influence was due, of course, largely to the general trend of the time. Actually, Danjūrō experimented on the stage with the new drama, and contributed to forming the new expression of the *Kabuki*. Danjūrō was skilled in oratory as well as in the delineation of psychology. As we have already seen in his presentation of *Ichinotani Futaba Gunki*, he tried to refine and spiritualize the *Kabuki*, and to add psychological presentation. In a word, he endeavored to pour as much new wine as possible into an old leather bag. The Meiji Restoration was not, however, as virginal a time for experiments in the *Kabuki*, as the Genroku era had been. Naturally, some of his experiments failed while others succeeded.

It was in 1894 that a play really deserving the

name of a new historical play was written by a playwright who had studied Western drama. It was *Kiri
Hitoha* (A Paulownia Leaf) by Tsubouchi Shōyō. Although this play was written especially for Danjūrō,
who was still active at the time, it was never presented
by him. Actually, it was not performed until ten
years later.

Since the turn of the century, new plays have
been written one after another. Of the many dramatists, Okamoto Kidō is the most outstanding. His
plays were written, under the influence of the free
theatre movement in France, for Ichikawa Sadanji the
Second, who introduced the plays of Ibsen to Japan.
Of his plays, the most famous ones are *Shuzenji Monogatari* (The Tale of Shuzenji), *Banchō Sarayashiki* (The
Plates of a Mansion in Banchō), *Toribeyama Shinjū*
(Toribeyama Double Suicide), etc. These plays are
written with a realistic technique, while at the same
time an attempt is made to keep as much of the *Kabuki*
form as possible. In that respect, his plays represent
a new movement for realism in the *Kabuki*. However,
in order that the *Kabuki* may become a true modern
drama, a still greater stride will have to be taken. It
does not, of course, mean that the *Kabuki* should
present plays which are concerned with people who
do not wear topknots, or that they should represent
the actual daily life of the present day. The question
is what new drama can be created upon the huge pile

of accumulated tradition. This problem has become more and more difficult as the gap between the *Kabuki* and the ever changing world, through the First and Second World Wars, has grown wider. At present the idea that the only thing that can be done with the *Kabuki* is to preserve the old form intact is most generally held. Preserving the *Kabuki* form, however, will still require that new plays will be written which can be presented by *Kabuki* actors, who are, after all, living human beings. It does not mean modernizing the play by breaking down the framework of the *Kabuki*. The difficulty lies, indeed, in beginning by reaffirming the *Kabuki* rather than by denouncing it. A serious task requiring expert art awaits new dramatists capable of coping with it.

## Chapter  IV

# *People  Who  Make  Up  the  Kabuki*

### 1.  People Who Appear on the Stage

In the performance of a drama, it is, of course, the actors who appear on the stage that impress the audience or appeal to them. That has always been the fundamental character of a drama in any country, as it is with the *Kabuki* in Japan. In no Western drama of any period, however, can one imagine people other than the actors appearing on the stage during the actual performance, making the audience wonder what their role or *raison d'être* might be. In a Shakespearean play, a man carrying a placard reading " This is Venice " may walk across the stage; but that man would really be considered one of the dramatis personae appearing there in order to explain the setting. During a *Kabuki* performance, however, people besides the actors appear on the stage and engage in various actions. The audience may wonder why those people are there, and may try to find a logical explanation of their existence on the stage, but they will not succeed. Thus, in a *Kabuki* performance, many people of various kinds appear on the stage;

this is a phenomenon which cannot be comprehended in the light of the European idea of a dramatic performance. If actors alone were supposed to appear on the stage, no *Kabuki* play could be performed.

In the *Kabuki* technique of dramatic presentation a play can be performed only when a number of people are engaged in a kind of protective firing, as it were, for each actor. Everything that can be handled behind the stage is of course handled there, but there are many things which an actor is unable to manage by himself on the stage, and for these he has to depend on the assistance of people who are not actors.

Song narration takes the place of the placard, mentioned above, which might be used in a Shakespearean play. By means of a little revolving stage, the song narrator appears in full view of the audience, together with his accompanist, on a platform to the right of the stage. As the play progresses, this person sings of the setting, the time, the situation, the relation between the dramatis personae, their emotions, etc. It is a kind of narration; but the narrator is actually there on the stage, and is therefore closely related to the actions of the actors. Sometimes this narrator speaks the lines for an actor, while the actor merely goes through the actions. Particularly, emotions are rendered fully and freely through this means, which is specially well adapted to the presentation of delicate or intense emotions, such as " a sorrow too deep for tears." The actor may clench his teeth and put on an expression of fierce agony while the narrator sings of his emotions for him. Suppose we apply this method to a Shakespearean play. "To be or not to be!" the narrator would sing, while the actor would go through actions suited to the words; and when the full attention of the audience is in this way centered upon him, the actor would then slowly bring out the next words, "That is the question!" This reciprocal or correlated action is part of the *Kabuki* technique.

In a *Kabuki* play, it very often happens that a person whom the audience has been led to take for a certain man would suddenly, in a particular situation, turn out to be a well-known historical figure, who had for some reason or other concealed his identity. In such a case, his wig and his costume would suddenly be changed, and, in most cases, he would be transformed into a powerful-looking personage. Now, an actor cannot accomplish this transformation all by himself. Assistants would have to appear on the stage to help the actor; and the audience would be expected to pretend that these assistants are invisible. The wig is changed into a different shape; pulling out threads would make the outer costume fall off, and from underneath a new costume would be revealed. Thus a character would be transformed on the spot into another person.

These assistants who appear on the stage with the

understanding that the audience consider them invisible are called *kurogo*. They are dressed in black from head to foot, and even their faces are concealed behind thin black cloth. They are not supposed to have any individual significance or personality on the stage. They arrange stage properties, do duty for a prompter, attend to minor changes in the lighting, look after the appearance and costumes of the actors on the stage, attend to sound and other effects and various stage tricks, and when a character " dies " on the stage they hold up a piece of black cloth, behind which the dead man can leave the stage without being seen by the audience. Such methods may be criticized as being too artificial, for it means that people on the stage have made a contract with the audience to regard visible things as invisible. When, in the course of the development of the *Kabuki*, plays of many scenes came to be demanded, the revolving stage was devised, and scene-shifters came on the stage and pushed the stage along to turn it about. In this device, too, the scene-shifters are supposed to be invisible. Also, when a plain curtain symbolizing " nothing " is unhooked and falls in a heap upon the stage—at some time during a scene when that change is required—the scene-shifters come on the stage in their Japanese equivalent of blue jeans—just as they are while working behind the stage—and carry the curtain away into the wing of the stage. Such complete indifference, on the part of the *Kabuki* producers, to trivial matters, or their supreme subjugation of them to the over-all effect, prompted the stylization of the *Kabuki*, and brought about the present degree of perfection in some of its aspects.

Even the front curtain used between acts is pulled along by a stage-hand and is concealed in the wing of the stage, instead of being raised upwards by mechanism. Furthermore, clappers are sounded while the curtain is being pulled, in order to add rhythm and an emotional appeal to the simple drawing of the curtain. This curtain, made of cotton, used to have several holes in it, through which the actors, who were already on the stage waiting for the opening of the curtain, used to take a look at the audience. Not only the actors, but also the scene-shifters, the people in charge of effects, and the young actors still in their training, all took a peep at the audience, which was indeed a peep from the world of the *Kabuki* into the real world. The audience, however, might already have assimilated themselves with the world of the *Kabuki*, and the tense atmosphere of their expectation might only have enticed the actors further away from reality.

## 2. How the *Kabuki* Was Made

When we speak of *Kabuki* plays we usually mean

old plays reproduced on the stage. It would seem that the *Kabuki* exists solely for the purpose of inheriting old classics, and of reproducing the same stage effects of the past. At least most *Kabuki* actors claim that reproduction of plays written before 1893—the year when the last of the *Kabuki* playwrights died—is the orthodox *Kabuki*. Fifty years ago, that is, in 1903— the year when, in the Western world, the Wright Brothers succeeded in flying in the air—two of the three greatest *Kabuki* stars of the modern era died. The people of the time, who had come in contact with the realistic stage of other countries, anticipated that the *Kabuki* would naturally fall into a steady decline leading to ultimate extinction. But the *Kabuki*, a form of drama which was born in the same age as that of Shakespeare, has lived on side by side with the drama of other nations ; and even now, in the latter half of the twentieth century, it has not only survived but enjoys ever increasing popularity among the Japanese.

In fact, the word *shibai* (play) in Japan even now refers, in a general sense, to the *Kabuki*. Western dramas—those by Ibsen, which are the classic dramas of the nineteenth century, or by the still earlier Molière, or even by Shakespeare, or even Greek drama—are called *shingeki* (the new drama), although no new idea of presentation is aimed at, and are regarded as the van- guard of drama in Japan. In other words, dramas whose themes are human beings, and dramas which deal with psychology or with social problems are called the new drama. This, however, is mainly a matter of appellation. Today, Japanese dramatists, producers, and prospective actors all study and train themselves in the Western drama and aspire to present it upon the stage. School dramatics is also confined almost entirely to the modern Western drama. Names alone remain unchanged; *shibai* in Japanese refers to the *Kabuki*, while Western-style drama is still called the " new drama."

The differentiation in names indicates that the *Kabuki* is a play whose main purpose is the development of the story. Furthermore, the story is conveniently constructed, and the main purpose in its presentation is to stress each scene and represent the vicissitudes in the circumstances, the situations, and the fates of the dramatis personae. The *Kabuki* concentrates exclusively upon showing the actors' actions on the stage to the greatest advantage in the highest effectiveness. In that sense, all *Kabuki* plays are well-made plays. By " well-made " we do not mean that they provide the audience with the interest and enjoyment of fiction by showing the changes in the situations. What we mean is that the *Kabuki* play is a script whose purpose is to provide the actors with chances to show themselves off.

In *Kabuki* plays, we find lines that convey hardly any sense, lines that are composed simply of adjectives, like the words of some of the latest " hit " songs. Indeed, the most famous lines in the plays are precisely those lines that convey little meaning. The *Kabuki* actors chant or speak those lines on the stage, entranced by the tone or ring of the passages, but not at all impressed or moved to sympathy by their purport. Such passages are requisite in *Kabuki* plays. Here lies the secret reason of the eternal reproduction or repeated performances of the same *Kabuki* plays. People do not look for sympathy for, or understanding of, the problems of life in the *Kabuki*. They expect to be carried into a trance, in which they may forget everything else in the atmosphere that is created upon the stage. The effect it produces is somewhat similar to that which is produced by *La Tosca* and *La Bohème*, which move Italians to shout in praise with tears flowing down their cheeks. We find many lines and actions which must have been added impromptu by some actors, just as in the *commedia dell'arte*. The actors of the *Kabuki* show a supreme sensitiveness in their actions which might equal the art of the ballet or Neue Tanz. They can even turn a somersault, when necessary, like a tumbler. They can walk the ropes like an acrobat, and they can fade out of sight in a puff of smoke. There are many scenes in the *Kabuki* of murder, of bloodshed, of poisoning, of agony, and of heads freshly cut off. These scenes, which remind one of the Grand Guignol of Paris, are favorites with *Kabuki* actors. The way in which pantomine, dancing, drama, and singing alternate on the stage in the *Kabuki* reminds one also of the " Chauve-Souris " of Nikita Balieff. Again the gorgeous gaiety of the *Kabuki* stage reminds one of a scene in a revue, such as Ziegfeld Follies. There are also scenes of utter silence in which a single paulownia leaf fluttering down upon the stage suddenly brings home to an aged warrier, who watches it, that the end of a reign is come—scenes that are sublimely philosophical in their monotony.

Thus, what the *Kabuki* aims at presenting is complex and varied. And in most parts the emphasis is laid not on the purport or significance but on form and pictorial beauty produced on the stage. For instance, thieves of various categories appear in *Kabuki* plays, but they are always thieves from the very beginning, and the reason for their being thieves and their methods of theft are always simple and conventional. They never resort to scientific methods as Arsène Lupin did. They are either nonchalant and audacious like gangsters or fidgety as mice.

Simple characters compose the dramatis personae of the *Kabuki*, and the actors try to present such characters in an attractive and interesting way through the development of situations. If we should look for delicate delineation of psychology in the *Kabuki* we would be disappointed. What the populace look for is the changes of the scenes on the stage, the living pictures, and the ecstasy of being immersed in a festive atmosphere. It is, therefore, much easier and less hazardous to pick out some old plays to perform than to look for new plays. The audience is satisfied with the reproduction of old plays ; indeed, they think that that is the real *Kabuki*.

Now, the old *Kabuki* plays are not reproduced in the same way that *Macbeth* would be repeated in a Western theatre today. They are not presented with any new objective ; they simply follow the traditional presentation. In most cases, the same actions to the same music that the *Kabuki* ancestors used are faithfully reproduced. The *Kabuki* reached a complete form about 350 years ago. In the course of these 350 years, great playwrights appeared now and then and wrote contemporary plays directly connected with the society of the time. Therefore, the *Kabuki* repertoire consists of numerous plays. New plays will naturally be required if the presentation of the contemporary man on the stage is what the audience demands. But, as we have seen, that is not what the populace who flock to the *Kabuki* require.

The preparations for a performance of a *Kabuki* play today are, therefore, very simple. As the play to be performed is perfectly familiar to everyone concerned, the speeches, the actions, the properties, the costumes, etc. are prepared in a twinkling. In fact, even if only four or five days are spent in the preparation of a new programme, all goes fairly well on the first day; and after the third day we may safely expect the whole thing to work as smoothly as if it had run for years in succession. But this was not the case in the days when the *Kabuki* was being created, when new plays were written and produced. A playwright would consult with the *zanushi*—corresponding to the producer—and decide on the subject, the story, the parts and scenes for each actor, and then sit down and write a play. In most cases, several playwrights wrote different scenes of the same play. These writers, as well as the actors, seem to have been in the habit of moving from one company to another at the beginning of each season, when a new programme for the year was being organized. When a play was finished, the owner of the company would read it to the *zamoto*, or *tayūmoto* (the producing manager), who would make necessary alterations, and then explain it to the head actor. In this way a new play was prepared.

The members of a company were not selected according to the play to be produced. The members were selected before the play was decided upon. The *tayūmoto*, the *chōmoto* (accountants), and other representatives of the three *Kabuki* theatres (only three *Kabuki* theatres used to be licensed in Tokyo) would meet once a year, and select actors for their respective companies. The names of all the actors

available were written on cards—one on each—
which were laid face down; and representatives of
the three companies took turns in picking up these
cards. That was how actors were allotted. The
yearly salaries of the actors were also decided upon at
this time.

One naturally wonders how a company composed
of members selected in such a haphazard fashion
could have a good working order. In the *Kabuki*, the
actors' roles are more or less fixed. There are the
*tachiyaku* (the actor for the principal male part), the
*onnagata* (actors for female roles), the *nimaime* (actors
for secondary male parts), the *akuyaku* (actors for
villains' parts), the *dōkeshi* (actors for comic roles),
the *babayaku* (actors for aged female parts—very important roles in the *Kabuki*), *jijiyaku* (actors for aged
men's roles), etc. As the allocation of actors was
made according to these different classes of actors,
it produced a well-formed company. A company
consisted of about 40 to 50 members. The most important business of the playwrights belonging to these
companies was to write a play that would make the
best use of all the actors thus assembled.

The first performance of the company was called
the *kaomise-kōgyō* (the face showing performance). A
ceremony called *kao-awase* (organizing ceremony) was
first held, when the new members drank to their
success; then they all together clapped their hands

— 101 —

nine times in three series of three clappings. Then
came the *hon-yomi* (reading of the play—which was
usually done by the playwright). The actors were not
provided with complete texts; only their respective
parts were copied for them, which were called the
*kakinuki* (extract). Then the *yomiawase* (reading out
the play), and the *tachigeiko* (rehearsing on foot) followed, in much the same way as a play would be rehearsed
today. However, in *Kabuki* rehearsals, a *furitsukeshi*
(coach—like the coach for a ballet dance) supervised
only scenes where correlated action by many people
was necessary. In other parts, each actor was left to
his own ingenuity. In the history of the *Kabuki* we
find no real director. The playwright may have performed part of the duties of a director, but he seldom
did more than what a stage-manager would be expected
to do. Neither does the head actor of a troupe seem
to have filled the place of a director, as in a performance of a Western classical drama. It would be more
correct to say that all the action and direction was left
to the individual actors.

Each individual actor not only worked out his
own action and his own speeches, but he also provided
his own costumes at his own expense. Although preliminary arrangement was made for the choice of
colors for the costumes, nobody knew what costumes
each actor would wear until the opening day. In the
*Kabuki* no dress-rehearsal was considered necessary.

How each actor would act was almost entirely unknown to the other actors until the first day. Therefore, the period of rehearsal was not a period for preparing or creating a performance, but was only a period when the actors' parts were allotted, and when they could only guess at the probable actions of each other. The rehearsals, naturally, were entirely different from the performance on the stage; they were based on guess-work. The lines did not have to be spoken aloud but could be mumbled in an undertone. The actions were simplified so that actors would waste no energy.

A long period of rehearsal was, therefore, un-necessary; in fact, the period seems never to have exceeded ten days at the most. It does seem very strange that a play could be performed in such a way. Indeed, there was a time, about 50 years ago, when the necessity for a longer period of rehearsal was voiced, as for Western dramas. But *Kabuki* actors merely laughed at the suggestion scornfully, according to documents of the time. The only explanation for their refusal to take such a suggestion seriously might be found in their great confidence in their own power to stir and sway the whole house on the very first day.

The majority of *Kabuki* actors were born to be actors; that is, they were born into actors' families, were brought up in the theatre, and were destined to grow up into actors. In older times, when there were no written plays, the actors put on a play by thinking out a story and arranging scenes verbally among themselves. Perhaps the actors themselves should have written the plays. Even after professional playwrights appeared, the actors probably considered it below their dignity to seem too anxious to rehearse plays which had been written by persons who were their subordinates.

Another reason why rehearsals were simple in the *Kabuki* is that the *Kabuki* play was not originally a play of speeches, but a play in which the most important thing was the development of situations which would show the talents of the individual actors. More emphasis was laid on how to sing the speeches than to express their meaning. Besides, the rhythm of the speeches was a very simple one, the lines being composed of a repetition of five and seven syllables. They were much easier to memorize than the lines of Western dramas. One Shakespearean play would take over twelve hours if it were to be performed by using the method of the *Kabuki*. Even today, the rehearsals of a *Kabuki* play are of short duration; only three or four days are spent in preparing plays for a ten hour program. Nevertheless, when the first day comes, each actor shows magic power and a well-organized performance is given.

Although the period of rehearsal is thus very short, the same piece is repeatedly performed, as in the opera. Many of the *Kabuki* pieces, in fact, have repeatedly been performed over a long period, during which a great number of different actors have acted the same piece over and over again year after year. When one actor improvises or adds a new device or a new form of presentation, that becomes part of the tradition which is handed down from generation to generation. Such new forms are handed down as the form of So-and-So; but in most cases, it does not refer to the individual actor but rather to the family of actors, which shows that one form of action has been worked on, refined, and crystallized, as it were, by generations of actors.

If one play has been acted over and over again for 350 years, one would naturally expect it to have reached a state of perfection, with all its deficiencies eliminated and all possible attractive features added. It would be only natural to expect that such a play, which has stood the criticism of the audiences and the populace, who are always the severest critics of drama in any country, should reveal in many parts a sublime refinement of presentation and a unique tone and flavor.

## 3. The Life of Actors

The majority of *Kabuki* actors are born into actors' families. They start learning to dance at the age of five or six. A great number of Japanese dances impersonate women, and since only men can become *Kabuki* actors, little boys destined to become actors learn feminine gestures through their lessons in Japanese dancing. Most of these Japanese dances were originally taken from *Kabuki* plays, and are still danced on the stage in *Kabuki* performances. Since there is this relation between *Kabuki* plays and Japanese dances, there is naturally a section of a *Kabuki* play that is similar to a movement in a Japanese dance. The boys are not trained in speaking lines. Instead, they are taught to sing the *jōruri* which was the foundation on which the *Kabuki* developed. In these narrations, there are speeches by men and women, old and young, and these have to be differentiated.

The only way the boys learn how to act is by watching their senior actors' performances for years. Until quite recently, little boys used to be seen, dressed in the *kurogo* (black gown), sitting patiently for hours in the wings of the stage, watching the stage intently. Such a practice seems to have died out. When a young actor is given an important role, or if he is given an unexpected part when the company goes on the road, he calls on a senior actor, whose favorite part it is, or an old actor whose favorite part it used to be, at his house, and asks him for personal instructions. The senior actor, or aged actor, on such occasions takes great pains to instruct the young actor in everything he himself knows about the part. In this way, an actor learns even a very big part in a few days, if he does not master it.

Now, one fatal problem for the *Kabuki* is that when a young actor learns a part from a senior actor in this way, he is bound by a sort of iron rule to act exactly as he has been taught to act that part. It would be considered a great breach of propriety if he should try to render his own conception of the part, or to reveal his own individuality. Times, however, are changing. Even if it is the rule for a young actor to act exactly as he has been instructed, he lives under different physical conditions from that of his seniors, and even if his brains are more or less the same, his thoughts are influenced by the age he lives in. Naturally, he will wish to act a part in his own way. The young actor will, however, act exactly as he had been taught if he perceives among the audience the senior actor who taught him, or anybody related to that senior actor. Thus a *Kabuki* actor's action is still more or less restricted by a traditional force.

A great change has taken place in the mode of life of *Kabuki* actors. Before the Meiji Restoration (1878), *Kabuki* actors were considered a separate class of people; they hardly belonged to ordinary society. Also, they had no connection with the upper classes, as not even the word " art " was known to them in those days. They existed exclusively for the populace.

At no time in its history has the *Kabuki* had patronage from the fashionable circles; nothing has existed that would correspond to the relationship between Shakespeare and Queen Elizabeth, or Molière and King Louis of France. The *Kabuki* has always been supported and patronized solely by the masses.

A *Kabuki* actor was easily distinguished on the streets; especially *onnagata* actors were conspicuous because of their feminine appearance, their gait, actions, and their feminine personal effects. Even in everyday life, they made up their faces and tried to be feminine. It was as if all their efforts were concentrated upon concealing the ill-luck of their having come into this world as men. Such a mode of life was possible for them only because these actors lived in their own exclusive society, cut off from the world; it was possible for them to be thorough-going in living like women. As for his private life, an *onnagata* might have a wife but most *onnagata* tried to conceal this fact. It is a historical truth that *onnagata* actors were extremely careful not to be seen with their wives, especially by the actors who were to be their lovers on the stage. They thought it would be highly improper if an *onnagata* should make his lover on the stage suddenly remember, in a love scene, that the woman he is in love with is really a man who has a wife. In the history of the *Kabuki* we find many cases of abnormality in the lives of *onnagata* actors. It was something beyond professional-consciousness; it was a peculiar pride they had in their destiny, a sort of pride a fatalist might harbor. If an *onnagata* should see the actor, who is to be his lover on the stage, talking happily in the corridor with a beautiful real woman, he would be filled with a kind of jealousy. When walking in the streets, an *onnagata* would be attracted by feminine objects, but would pay no attention to men's things. Such " peculiar " people have been the essential element of the *Kabuki*. A sense of self-sacrifice, of subjugating one's will, was required of the *onnagata*; they were to live solely for the *Kabuki* tradition. But times are changing, and such self-sacrifice is growing more and more difficult.

A young man talking with his friend in a coffee-shop down-town looks at his Swiss-made wrist-watch, jumps to his feet, and cries in colloquial language: " Gosh! It's time. I've got to go." He dashes out, catches a taxi, and is gone. There is nothing peculiar about him. He is just an ordinary young city-bred man. This young man walks into the theatre through the stage-door. A *gesokuban* (man who takes care of foot-gear) places for him a pair of *zōri* (straw sandals), which the young man puts on after removing his shoes. He, then, walks down the passage of wooden floor. On one side is the *tōdori-beya* (the back-stage manager's room), in the window of which is placed the " arrival board " (a board on which the names of actors are written and which has a small hole above each name). The young man picks up a tiny bamboo peg which he inserts into the hole above his own name. This is the "time recorder." The *tōdori* says, "Good morning," and the young man returns the greeting by also saying, "Good morning." Whatever time of the day it might be— morning, noon, or night—the greeting exchanged between people behind the stage is always "Good morning" when they meet, and "*Otsukare-san*" (Good rest) when they part. The young man walks on along a passage, which reminds one of a passage in a hospital. He passes by a fairly spacious room with open doors, in which brave looking warriors with strange make-up, dressed in their costumes, and beautifully dressed princesses of the feudal ages can be seen. This room, provided with a large mirror, is the waiting-room for actors who are ready to go on the stage. When one realizes that these warriors and princesses are really men living in the present age, one feels an eerie sensation, which comes from the supernatural world in which a *Kabuki* play is performed.

The room into which the young man enters is a fine Japanese-style room, with an ante-room attached to it. This room is separated from all the other rooms. Several pupils of his, who are to wait on him, greet him in unison with the above mentioned "Good morning," to which he returns the same greeting in a casual tone. He is no longer the same young man who was chatting with his friend in the coffee-shop only a short while ago. He has become an entirely different man. Removing his *zōri*, he walks into the room. He throws off his Western suit, and puts on a *yukata* (cotton *kimono*). A pupil offers him a cup of tea. While he is sipping the tea, another pupil comes in to announce that the bath is ready. The young man leaves his room. While he is gone, his pupils put his room in order and set out his costumes and the property he is to carry. Presently the young man returns with a flushed face after a hot bath, and squats in front of a large mirror. Another cup of tea is brought to him. While drinking tea he glances through his fan letters, and chats with his pupils. One of his pupils, who has been watching the progress of the program, comes in to inform the young man that it is time to get ready. All of a sudden the young man becomes serious in his whole attitude, as he gazes intently at his own face in the mirror. "*Yoshi!*" (Ready!) he calls. That is a signal for the beginning of his make-up. He pulls his *yukata* down to his waist, and his pupils paint his neck and back thickly.

After binding his head with a cloth band, he greases his face, and then applies white paint all over his face with a brush. *Kabuki* actors never use Hollywood style toilet articles; they stick to the traditional

— 111 —

*Kabuki* make-up. Then he very carefully applies red, black, and green paints to his eyes, nose, mouth, eyebrows, cheeks, temples, and ears, using his finger-tips, his palm, and various kinds of brushes. When all his make-up is finished, he calls aloud in the direction of the ante-room. The *ishōya* (costume man) now comes in and puts on him the costume of a medieval Japanese woman, squeezing him tight. During this time the pupil who is watching the stage comes in from time to time to inform the actor how far the play has progressed. Now here stands a woman of old Japan, except for the top of the head, which still reveals a boy's hair.

Next the *tokoyama* (wig man) comes in with a wig. The young actor puts his hands to his ears, which is a signal for the wig man to put the big heavy-looking wig upon the actor's head. The actor removes his hands, with which he has been holding the bottom of the wig. Simultaneously, the wig man presses the wig forward from behind. The young man has now turned into a woman from head to toe. Various gay-colored hair-ornaments are thrust into the wig from the left and the right and from the front.

A pupil comes in to say it is very near the time he, no, she, has to go on the stage. Still unperturbed he—she—extracts a cigarette from a package of Lucky Strikes placed in front of the mirror. Smoking it, he turns again to the mirror, and pulls up his sleeves.

While a pupil holds his sleeves from behind, he picks up a brush again and paints thickly his hands, his arms, and even his hairy shanks, in order to make these parts match the color of his face. All this manipulation for bringing about a complete transformation of the young man has not taken more than half an hour at the most. On the *tatami* (mat) at the door of his room are placed his foot-gear for the stage. He stands up and once more looks intently at his own image in the mirror from a little distance. He himself seems to be fascinated by the beautiful woman in the mirror. Now holding up the long skirt of his costume in one hand, he walks out of his room, followed by his pupils who carry his cup of tea, his parasol, stick, and so forth.

The sound of clappers is heard from the stage. Passing through a corridor, he comes to the back of the stage, and then goes down the steps into the basement, where he proceeds along a narrow passage. In what is called the *Naraku* (Hell) right under the stage, he passes by the electric mechanism of the revolving stage. He also passes by the apparatus for lifting an actor up onto a part of the *hanamichi* called *shichi-san*. Passing right below the audience, he reaches another staircase, which he mounts. Now he is in a small room at the back of the hall, with a mirror on one wall. He does not sit down on the chair offered him by a janitor, but remains standing. This room is

— 113 —

separated from the house only by a thin wall. It must be an interval now; a distant din, like the clamor of a huge mass of people, is heard.

Now comes the sound of clappers from the direction of the stage—a signal for the opening of the curtain. The whole house is suddenly hushed. More sounds of clappers—loud and clear, drawing the full attention of the audience to the stage. The curtain opens. A stir of expectation sways the audience. Then comes the deep bass of the song-narration, accompanied by *samisen* music.

The young actor drains in one draught the cup of tea held out by his pupil, and holding all his property in his hands, he faces a small curtain, fully prepared to emerge. At a signal by music, the janitor swiftly pulls aside the little curtain, which is called the *agemaku*. The curtain rings make a slight sound, which is nevertheless heard by all the audience, who turn their gazes with one accord from the stage to the entrance of the *hanamichi*, waiting in a hush of suspense for the actor's appearance.

Delicately, gracefully, he moves towards the stage, to the rhythm of the music. He is something sublimely remote from all reality. The whole house stirs. Sighs of adoration rise. His professional name is called from every corner of the house, intermingled with the cries: " There you come! " The actor slowly approaches the stage, his whole movement suggestive of a suppressed response to the cries and the stirring among the audience.

## 4. Actors and Audience

Nearly all *Kabuki* actors are hereditary. At a certain age, with a grand ceremony, they inherit the title of the family together with the huge debts that run in all actors' families. Patrons of the *Kabuki* are also very often hereditary, generations of one family patronizing generations of a certain actors' family. Such a patron buys a certain number of tickets, not only for the introduction performance of the actor, but also for each month that his actor plays. An actor with a great number of such patrons has a good chance of success. He is better liked by the *zanushi* and is given better roles. Fame, therefore, is also hereditary in the *Kabuki* world. Being born into a distinguished family of actors is the only way to fame. Adoption by such a family hardly guarantees success; much less can an actor of no name hope to achieve anything approaching fame, no matter how hard he may try. In short, a *Kabuki* actor needs the support of play-goers. No amount of talent or skill by itself can bring him fame or success. There has hardly been any case, in the long history of the *Kabuki*, in which mere talent or diligence brought popularity to an actor. Popularity is achieved by the family title and by the support of play-goers.

A true patron is always liberal in trying to increase the popularity of his actor—though a change of conditions after the Second World War has nearly extinguished such patrons—and he even looks after the family finances of the actor. Such strong intimate support may seem strange and incomprehensible to people familiar only with the Western tradition of drama or with cinema fans. It is not implied here that there are no *Kabuki* fans ; there are a great number of them, among the young as well as the old. It is indeed interesting to note that the *Kabuki* has come into great vogue recently among teen-age girls. Why should young people of today be interested in plays created centuries ago—plays with illusory and often absurd stories? The answer is that the *Kabuki* has not ceased to provide the majority of modern Japanese people with the pleasure which seems to come from the re-affirmation of the old feudal morals of *giri* (duty) and *ninjō* (natural human feelings), a clash of which is the basic theme of *Kabuki* plays.

Because the *Kabuki* has lived with the Japanese people for centuries, there are some play-goers who know more about *Kabuki* plays—though their knowledge is strictly from the point of view of the audience —than the actors. Such people, who are called the *tsū* (connoisseurs), have loved the *Kabuki* with unceasing fidelity, and have made the *Kabuki* a part of their lives. Such people, indeed, may have been the mainspring which has supported and sustained the *Kabuki* all these years.

In former days, *Kabuki* theatres used to have two passages, called the *hon hanamichi* and the *kari hanamichi* (cf. Chap. II), running parallel through the audience's seats to the stage. In some plays they were supposed to be the two banks of a river; in other plays they were a continuation of the same highway. In a certain well-known play, there used to be a place where an actor coming down the *kari hanamichi* walked between the audience's seats and reached the *hon hanamichi* while, on the stage, the revolving stage was turned about and the scene was shifted. Once during a performance of this play an actor carrying his bundle had come off the *kari hanamichi* and, passing among the audience, was about to reach the *hon hanamichi*, when someone in the audience suddenly called to him, holding out a cup of *sake*, saying, " You must be tired. Do rest a while. How about a drink? " The actor who happened to dislike alcohol, declined the offer and replied, " I would rather have some sweets," whereupon, the man produced a *manjū* (bean-jam bun) and said, " Then please take this." So the actor accepted it and proceeded up the *hon hanamichi*, eating the bun; and having reached the stage, which had been shifted in the meantime, he continued with his performance. After that, every time the actor reached this identical

— 117 —

spot, something was offered him, although the audience was different each day; and the actor was somewhat dismayed, as he could not very well refuse. This episode shows the kind of intimacy that used to bind the audience to the actors. The audience was unmistakably an important element that made up the *Kabuki*.

Nowadays, however, the audience is made up largely of people who go there in parties. Under such circumstances, it has become very difficult to maintain the peculiar atmosphere of the *Kabuki* theatre. These parties are made up of people who were given complimentary tickets by some firms. The number of such people is really very great. It is as if parties of fifty or sixty people had come on a picnic to the theatre; they look happiest when they are eating lunch in the restaurant in the theatre. People who really go to the theatre of their own choice to see the *Kabuki* plays are consequently very few in number. Thus the audience is changing with the change of times. The *Kabuki* itself may change accordingly. Whether the result will be a new development in the art, or whether it will bring about its collapse, depends not so much on the *Kabuki* actors, nor the playwrights, nor the management, but on the taste and the power of the two hundred thousand people who monthly flock to the *Kabuki* theatres.

## Chapter  V
# The Kabuki and Contemporary Japan

In the Tokugawa era, the *Kabuki* was " contemporary drama," liked and loved by the populace of Japan, for it was closely connected with the life of the people.  For instance, an actual case of double suicide was at once dramatized into a " double suicide play," and was duly performed ; it was even said that double suicide plays had set the fashion for double suicides. After the Meiji Restoration, however, the *Kabuki* lost its close touch with the populace, and in the theatres in great cities it gradually grew into a peculiar genre of drama appreciated by special connoisseurs and people of fashionable circles.

There are some cases, on the other hand, in small towns and farming villages, where the *Kabuki* still survives in very much the same form it had .in the Tokugawa era.  In some of these villages there are old playhouses, and the people of the whole community are in one way or another connected with the plays that are performed there.  The actors are mostly volunteers from among the village people.  Instead

of being paid for acting, they pay their own expenses.
The person who gets the best part pays the most.
The performances are given at the annual village
festival. They are also given, on a smaller scale, on
other occasions. These village *Kabuki* performances,
however, cannot be said to be more popular than other
kinds of popular entertainment, such as the movies,
for instance.

According to surveys made at regular intervals of
the audiences of Japanese theatres, 70 to 80 per cent
of the audience who go to the *Kabuki* Theatre in
Tokyo are people over thirty years of age, whereas
70 to 80 per cent of the people who go to see modern
plays are in their teens or in their twenties. This
fact seems to show that the *Kabuki* no longer appeals
to the younger people today. The majority of the
audience of the *Kabuki* Theatre in Tokyo are people
who have been invited by business firms, etc., and
only a minor part of the audience consists of true
*Kabuki* lovers who come of their own choice. One
cause of such a phenomenon is that the tickets for the
*Kabuki* theatres in Tokyo and Osaka are too expensive
for the populace to buy them. The real *Kabuki* lovers
can manage to buy tickets only for the " peanut "
gallery. In smaller cities and towns, however, when
the Tokyo or Osaka *Kabuki* make a tour of the country,
most of the audience come of their own initiative,
because, for one thing, they seldom have a chance to

see the real *Kabuki*. Among traditional Japanese dramas, the *Kabuki* still has a wider range of appeal and larger audiences than the *Noh* drama or the *Kyōgen*.

The *Kabuki* has been for a long time a place where society people congregate. It has always been closely connected with the gay quarters, and a great number of the women in the *Kabuki* audience belong to the gay quarters. In many cases, they have been the medium through which their customers of the upper class have become *Kabuki*-goers. Many *Kabuki* actors are teachers of Japanese dancing; they are also often related to players of Japanese music. As a matter of fact, Japanese dancing and Japanese music are correlative arts.

As we have already seen, the *Kabuki* was the drama of the people in the Tokugawa era, and there was naturally a close relationship between the stage and the audience. One remnant of the practises of the era is the custom for people in the audience to shout to the actors at climactic moments. They call out the family name of the actor, or shout, " *Matte mashita!* (There you come!)," " *Daitōryō!* (Great leader)," " *Nippon ichi!* (Japan's best)," etc. These shouts come mostly from the " peanut " gallery where the true *Kabuki* fans are seated. *Kabuki* fans are fond of listening to the mimicry of actors' speeches. The origin of such mimicry was the custom for actors to parade the streets of a town for preliminary advertisement. Later, mimics became independent professionals, and performed in Japanese vaudevilles. Today such mimicry is often broadcast, and is popular with *Kabuki* fans. This is another peculiarity of the *Kabuki* which is not found in modern drama.

Since the end of the Second World War, however, the *Kabuki* has come to be somewhat more popular than before among younger people. Every well-known university in Tokyo has its own *Kabuki* Study Club, but the activities of such clubs are limited to the study of the *Kabuki*, and performances by a small group of students, who constitute a very small per cent of Japanese youths.

Although the *Kabuki* today may no longer be as popular as it used to be, something of the ideas and feelings presented in the *Kabuki* drama, and some manners and customs that are peculiar to the *Kabuki* still persist in the lives of the average Japanese. Present-day life in Japan is a combination of the modern and the old. Contrasts are seen in manners and physical things, as well as in spiritual life, in thoughts and feelings.

One of the most apparent persistent influences of the *Kabuki* is seen in the *kimono*. Patterns of the clothes which actors of the Edo era wore on the stage are still the most commonly used patterns of the *kimono*. For instance, the *ichimatsu* pattern used for a *kimono* as well as for a *fusuma* (a paper sliding door) was originally the pattern of the clothes worn by Ichimatsu, a *Kabuki* actor in the Tokugawa era. Ever since he used it on the stage, it has been a popular pattern among the people of Japan.

The dramatis personae who appear on the *Kabuki* stage today express the ideas and feelings of the old Japan, but the majority of the Japanese audience are, nevertheless, moved to deep sympathy by the speeches and actions. It shows that the ancient Japan still lives in the life and culture of the present-day Japanese. The story of a *Kabuki* play is most frequently built around the central themes of loyalty to one's lord and filial piety, which were the bases of Japanese feudalistic morality. There are stories of how a *samurai* would die on the battlefield, or sacrifice his own family, or spend long years in search of his late master's enemy in order to avenge his master, etc., as acts of supreme self-sacrifice to serve his lord and master, in return for the kindness and care he had received at his master's hand. There are also many famous *Kabuki* dramas in which a parent sacrifices his own child for the sake of his master, as in " Kumagai Jinya," described at the beginning of this book, and in *Terakoya*.

In the *Forty-seven Rōnin*, still one of the most popular *Kabuki* dramas, the forty-seven retainers of a lord disguise themselves as men of various occupations and spend a whole year spying out the interior conditions and constructions of the enemy's residence, and finally succeed in avenging their master's death. Since the Japanese people even today emphasize the distinction of social standing in their human relationships,* the act of loyalty performed on the stage stirs a feeling of deep admiration in the minds and hearts of the Japanese people, at least of those who are above middle age. A young salaried man at a performance of the *Forty-seven Rōnin*, when asked what he thought of the loyalty depicted on the stage, answered: " I think it is only natural that one should serve one's firm, or one's employer, with the same kind of loyalty as that of the ' forty-seven men.' " That is only one example, but it shows that the ideas of unconditional submission to one's superiors and of self-sacrificing service stir a feeling of sympathy even in the young Japanese of today.

The idea of returning the kindnesses one owes is seen in the concept of filial piety in the relations between parent and child. The ideal of filial piety is that the child should obey his parent and be ready to sacrifice himself for his parent. For instance, the play titled *Nijūshikō* tells the story of a child who searches in the snow for bamboo shoots in winter because his mother expressed the wish to taste a bamboo shoot.

In the *Kabuki* there are also plays dealing with

* It is commonly expected that a person of lower standing should serve his superior with something of the old loyalty and submission.

the love of the parent toward the child. There are many plays, for example, in which the mother grieves over the hard fate which will not allow her to reveal her identity, for some complicated reasons, when she meets her child from whom she has been separated for years. In fact, this is a very popular theme in the movies today. Movies dealing with the tearful separation of mother and child, or with a mother who cannot reveal herself to her own child, constitute a special genre of movies. They are called the " mother stories," or " tearful stories."

The foundation of both the virtues of loyalty and of filial piety is the idea of *on* (a debt of gratitude). *On* is the debt which an inferior owes his superior. In the case of a *samurai*, it is the debt he owes his lord ; the people owe a debt to the nation ; a child owes a debt to his parents. The idea of paying that debt, as it is presented in the *Kabuki*, lies in the deepest corners of Japanese minds and hearts, if not clearly and consciously felt or expressed.

In the old ethical code of the Japanese people, there is also the idea of knowing one's place, of keeping oneself within one's place and never exceeding one's place or position. It is a virtue that was required in the feudal society where a caste system was rigidly maintained. This idea still survives as *giri* (obligation) and restricts the social activities of the Japanese people in various ways. *Giri* requires that a person should act in strict accordance with his place or position. For instance, the *giri* between a master and a subordinate means that the master should act like a master, and that the subordinate should act like a subordinate. And this *giri* sustains the mutual relation between the master and the subordinate—the love of the master for his subordinate, and the loyalty of the subordinate toward his master. *Giri* also manifests itself in the sense of honor, and emphasis is laid on dignity. A person owes himself the debt of keeping up his dignity, of not disgracing his name. Japanese people in the old days sacrificed themselves for these ideas of *giri*, as well as for *on*. A person might commit suicide out of a sense of *giri* to somebody else; or he might commit suicide in order to save his dignity. In the *Chūshingura* a *samurai* commits suicide from a sense of responsibility as he is mistakenly convinced that he has killed his father-in-law. In another play, a lady attendant of a *daimyō* commits suicide from a sense of shame because she was insulted and struck by the chief lady-in-waiting.

The feudalistic shackles of *on* and *giri*, which are presented in the *Kabuki*, often clash with *ninjō*, (natural human feelings). This conflict is most frequently the cause, or theme, of the tragedy. In " Kumagai," and in *Terakoya*, the scenes where the parents, who sacrifice their children, are torn between their sense of loyalty and their love for their children are the scenes which appeal to the audience's sympathy and move them to tears. *Sendaihagi* is a tragedy in which the nurse of an infant lord makes her own child eat poison in place of the young lord. This play is a representative *Kabuki* tragedy based on the mother's conflict between her natural grief and her loyalty. One reason for the great attraction the *Kabuki* has for the Japanese people is the fact that such a tragedy of conflict is continually repeated in the actual lives of the Japanese people in the clashes between the love of the family and the sense of duty to one's superiors outside the family. One characteristic of the *Kabuki* tragedy, indeed, is that it is brought about by a conflict between the conventions of the old society and human feelings. In the *Kabuki* there is no tragedy of fate or of character comparable to that of the Western drama. Many " double-suicide plays " in the *Kabuki* are tragedies of the conflicts between the laws and customs of an old society and human nature, for the young men and women commit " double suicide " in order to consummate their love through death when feudalistic conventions prohibit their marriage in this life.

It is not merely the feudalistic morals and acts in the *Kabuki* plays that stir a feeling of sympathy in the hearts of the audience ; it is rather the efforts and struggles of these people to reassert human nature within the framework of feudalistic morals that appeals most deeply to them. Thus, the *Kabuki*, while presenting on the stage the lives of the people of old Japan, is not, for the majority of present-day Japanese, mere reminiscences of past events and people, but also contains many elements which are familiar to the people today. In this sense, the *Kabuki* plays are not mere historical plays; they contain a significance closely related to the life and feelings of the modern Japanese. Even if the life of the Japanese people becomes more modernized in the future, the *Kabuki* tragedy of human nature will still impress and move the people.

## Chapter VI

# The Position of the Kabuki in the Cultural History of Japan

It is usually asserted that the *Kabuki* as a specific form of drama made its appearance in the history of Japan in the year 1603.   But, as with other forms of drama, the *Kabuki* could not have suddenly been born of nothing.   In the process of its development, it incorporated various elements of the *Noh*, the *Kyōgen*, and other dramas that preceded it, all of which in their turn were influenced by dramas of ancient and medieval Asiatic countries, especially, perhaps, of China and south eastern countries.   These elements make up the background of the *Kabuki*, out of which came its unique form;  and no one, therefore, can possibly say that it came into being in this or that year.   However, the year 1603 still has some importance because in that year a certain Okuni, a young, half-legendary *miko* (a maiden serving in a shrine) of a large shrine in the Province of Izumo, went up to Kyoto, the capital of the country then, and gave a performance of *Kabuki* dances for the first time in history.   This early *Kabuki*, which consisted of simple songs and simple dances accompanied by simple music, in a very short period of time developed into a full-fledged drama with dialogues and acting.

The year 1603, memorable in England for the death of Queen Elizabeth and the first publication of Shakespeare's *Hamlet*, was the first year of the Tokugawa government—which, incidentally, was the last of the feudal governments in Japan—Iyeyasu having established his *bakufu* (military government) in Edo in that year. Between that year and 1868, when the Shogunate came to an end and the Meiji Restoration was accomplished, the *Kabuki* play for two centuries and a half of the Edo era had continually been improved until it reached a superb form, consummate as a type of drama. In considering the position of the *Kabuki* in the cultural history of Japan, it is not enough to note how the *Kabuki* attained a perfection of form during those two centuries and a half; the important thing is to realize that the Edo era was a unique era in the history of the whole world, and that the *Kabuki* which developed in that era had, consequently, a unique quality.

The Edo era is often called the age of seclusion, as the government closed the nation's doors to almost all foreign countries. After Shogun Iyeyasu came to power, communications with other countries soon became closely regulated, and commercial intercourse with all foreign countries except Holland and China was prohibited. And even the favored Dutch, the only European traders with Japan, were required to live in a limited quarter of a sea-port town in the western part of Japan. This small ventilator through which the culture of Holland, and European culture by way of Holland, might have poured in was made yet smaller by means of strict censorship. This state of seclusion lasted until the end of the Edo era.

Thus the *Kabuki* play originated and developed in the secluded Japan, all but cut off from any direct influence of foreign culture. This situation was certainly very unusual and perhaps has no parallel in the modern drama of any country. This peculiar circumstance has placed the *Kabuki*, as a classical form of drama, in an unusual position in modern Japan since the Meiji Restoration. Clearly, there is a great difference between the significance in the present day world of the European classical dramas of Shakespeare, Racine, Corneille, and Molière and that of the *Kabuki*. What is this difference? One who tries to generalize very boldly, and a little carelessly, may declare that, whereas Shakespeare and Molière are " contemporary dramas " in the sense that they still appeal strongly to the audience of today, the *Kabuki* is merely a " drama of the past," a beautiful inheritance from old days, which may enchant and intoxicate one with its beauty but cannot have any direct and forceful appeal to the contemporary audience. This assertion, although it is far too bold and too superficial, contains a certain amount of truth which we must admit when we consider the *Kabuki* in comparison with European classical dramas. We may begin by considering why such a negative idea of the significance of the *Kabuki* can be entertained, for this may lead us to a clear idea of the whole problem of the *Kabuki* drama.

The state of seclusion, in which the *Kabuki* accomplished its spectacular development, may well be likened to an iron tube, both ends of which are tightly closed, which lies at the bottom of a river. In the river many kinds of waterplants grow, various fishes live, and the water flows rapidly on. The form of the river-bed is constantly altered by the rapid flow of the water. Undoubtedly various changes also take place in the iron tube; in its pent-up water some kinds of duckweeds grow, microbes swim, and the water itself changes—but all these things are entirely unrelated to what is happening in the wider world outside the tube. One can easily imagine the chaos into which Japan was thrown when after about three centuries of seclusion the stopper was removed and the culture of the wider world—chiefly European in this case—poured into the tube. The essential quality of this chaos, to put it in a few words, was a consternation caused by the tremendous difficulty of reconciling Japanese culture, (which had developed with no contact with the outer world for almost three centuries,)

with the European culture which had suddenly started pouring into the country.

As far as external, or material, things were concerned, there was no insurmountable difficulty in reconciling the two by replacing the old with the new.
For instance, in the case of lighting equipment, sub-
stitution of gas and electric lights for candles and
rape-seed oil lamps could be accomplished with
reasonable promptness and facility, though, as a matter of fact, the establishment of facilities for generating
gas and electricity, so unrelated to anything in the past
history of the country, was enough to engender
further confusion in the life of the people. We may
easily imagine the greatness of the perplexities when
we realize that these material things, which were the
results of ages of inventions and experimentations that
had gone on in the European countries now ready to
achieve an industrial revolution, were suddenly trans-
planted to Japan which had lived and developed with
no knowledge whatever of the progress of these inventions in Europe. It was only natural that great
confusion at the disruption with the past should
ensue.

But now let us return to drama and see what
happened there. It was at the turn of the century
that the new movement of modern drama in Europe,
heralded by André Antoine's " Théâtre Libre " in
Paris around 1880, was introduced into Japan. About

— 133 —

the same time two outstanding figures, Shōyō Tsubouchi and Kaoru Osanai, tried, independently, to ini-
tiate a modern-drama movement in Japan. Tsubouchi organized a group named the " Literary Association," and Osanai formed another in great enthusiasm
named the " Liberty Theatre." The first play the
former group staged was *Hamlet*, and Ibsen's *John
Gabriel Borkman* was the first one put on by the latter
group. These two enthusiastic leaders, however, were
confronted with the utter impossibility of finding
Japanese actors to play in these dramas, for the only
drama that existed in Japan was the *Kabuki* drama,
although there did exist, and still does exist, a form
of drama called " the new drama." This " new
drama " of the period was merely a variation of the
*Kabuki*, for it was essentially the same as the *Kabuki* in
its technique of acting, stage production, and playwriting, the only significant difference being the re-
placement of the old *Kabuki* costumes and manners
(topknots and swords, for instance) with those of the
Meiji era. So it can be said that the only drama
existing in Japan in those days was the *Kabuki*. In the
preceding chapters it has been made clear that it is
next to impossible to convey the meaning of Shakespeare or Ibsen with the acting techniques of the
*Kabuki* actors. Therefore, Tsubouchi, seeing that the
only way in which he could possibly begin a new drama
movement was to use completely new actors, opened

a school of drama, trained amateur college graduates, and staged *Hamlet*. Osanai, on the other hand, finding himself obliged to use *Kabuki* actors in presenting *Borkman*, made the best of the situation by using young Ichikawa Sadanji who had just returned from a trip through Europe and who had the newest ideas *Kabuki* actors could have been expected to have. Neither of these men, in spite of their earnest intentions, achieved very much, for Tsubouchi himself, born in the Edo era and educated in the ancient philosophy of Confucius, had had all his dramatic training in the world of the *Kabuki*; and Osanai, though he was nearly twenty years younger than Tsubouchi, and though he digested modern European philosophy much more thoroughly than Tsubouchi did, suffered under the decisive disadvantage of having to depend solely on *Kabuki* actors, although he did find one who possessed ideas comparatively modern for the period.

However that may have been, the modern drama movement in Japan took its first faltering step with these men, and it has by now developed into a form not much inferior to that of any nation. The new movement started at the moment when it broke away from the classic *Kabuki* drama—at the moment, in other words, when it had to divorce itself entirely from the traditional drama of the country and start building a new form of its own, with its foundation laid in modern European drama. It will be easily imagined what confusion accompanied the attempt to transplant suddenly the results of modern European drama, which had been born and nurtured in Europe, into Japan which had had nothing whatever to do with the development of European drama.

In Europe, though there are two forms of drama, the classical drama and the modern drama, the same actors play in both. For instance, Sir Laurence Olivier who played Henry V in a Shakespearean drama during one season plays the Duke of Altair in Christopher Fry's *Venus Observed* during the next; and Miss Mildred Dunnock who played in Arther Miller's *Death of a Salesman* last year may be found playing in a drama by Molière this year. In Japan there are also two forms of drama, the classical drama, the *Kabuki*, and the modern drama—the *shingeki* (lit., the "new drama.") They are, however, performed by two distinctly different groups of actors—the *Kabuki* actors and the *shingeki* actors. The *shingeki* actors are more or less similar to the actors of European countries; they perform modern Japanese dramas as well as dramas of other countries—of Shakespeare, Molière, Calderón, Goethe, Tennessee Williams, etc. The only difference is that the European actors have in their repertory both modern and classical dramas of their own countries, but the new-drama actors in Japan do not have the *Kabuki* in their repertory; the *Kabuki* is played only by *Kabuki* actors ; and the *Kabuki* actors, as a rule, perform no modern dramas.

The relationship between the classical drama (the *Kabuki*) and the modern drama (the *shingeki*) in Japan is qualitatively different from that in Europe. A good example of this is observed in the technique of utterance ; when *Kabuki* actors deliver a declamation, they use a method of utterance different from what the Japanese use today in their daily conversation, while the utterance of *shingeki* actors are essentially those of daily conversation. In European classical dramas the utterance of a declamation (although it is as exaggerated as in the *Kabuki*) is an extension of everyday conversation ; when the voice used in daily life is trained they become the utterance in classical dramas, and the training of voices in classical dramas is at once the basic training for modern ones. On the contrary, not only can voice-training in the *Kabuki* not be used as the basic training for actors of a modern play in Japan, but it even does them harm.

As has already been indicated, the *Kabuki* is a product of the Edo era, a feudal period in which Japan's doors were closed to the outer world ; and the mind of the people were also closed. It is natural that the plays of the *Kabuki* reflect the peculiar conditions of that era. The early part of the Edo era correspond in period of time to the Renaissance in Europe when modern bourgeois society was already established, or was in the process of being established. It is natural, then, that the significance the European dramas of the Renaissance have in the present-day world is different from what the *Kabuki* dramas have; and we see that the assertion that the *Kabuki* is a " drama of the past " while the classical European drama is a " contemporary drama " is in large part true. On the other hand, however, this still seems too bold and too careless a conclusion. Of course, there is a gap between the modern and the pre-modern ages in Japan. However, no one can overlook the fact that the Japanese have been in existence generation after generation from pre-modern days until the present moment. In other words, metaphorically speaking, a lamp burning rape-seed oil is a kind of light, just as an electric lamp is. To the Japanese of today is assigned a difficult task : how can life be brought back to this special form of classical drama, the *Kabuki*, in this present age, and how can the classical and modern be unified? For an effort to meet this task, nothing is more important than a thorough understanding of the position the *Kabuki* holds in the cultural history of Japan.

If we fail to grasp the historical significance of the *Kabuki* drama, and, being fascinated merely by its gorgeous beauty and the different possibilities it suggests, attempt at random to transplant its various elements into another form of drama, we shall not contribute to a real development of this superb classical drama. In fact, every aspect of present-day culture is laboring to bridge the gap between old traditional patterns and modern importations—in short, to bring about a rational unification of the cultural inheritance. The terms "tradition" and the "inheritance of tradition" in Japan comprise a peculiar and a much more complex meaning than they do in Western countries. And the problems arising from this question of the cultural heritage defy simple solution. As a matter of fact, although the problem of how the *Kabuki* may be made to function as present-day drama has been widely discussed, particularly in recent years, among critics, historians, and dramatists, no conclusion has been reached. It is a problem which will take years of experimentation before it can reach any solution. I should like, therefore, in this connection, to satisfy myself by merely relating my own opinions on the subject as a dramatist actually engaged in the task of writing modern drama, who is at the same time profoundly interested in the *Kabuki*.

As I have explained in the foregoing pages, the *Kabuki* was born and developed in the feudal Edo era, which was an era of seclusion. Consequently, the classical *Kabuki* plays performed today reflect the typical thoughts and feelings of a feudal era. The themes of most of these dramas are the acceptance and glorification of the absolute loyalty to one's lords and parents, and the unconditional submission to the

— 139 —

bondage of the "family." At the same time, however, the best of the *Kabuki* plays, perhaps accidentally, reveal the agonizing sorrows of the human soul that must resist the unconditional surrender of itself, while on one hand they decidedly do accept and glorify the feudal virtues. The *Kabuki* actors have mastered, through long years of training, the remarkable technique of artistic exaggeration by which they convey all such emotions—the acceptance and glorification of the feudal virtues and the agony of the instinctive resistance against such virtues. Such elements of the *Kabuki* are, moreover, intertwined with certain conditions on the part of the audience, which further add to the complexity of the situation. Many aspects of feudalism still remain unresolved in the life of the present-day Japanese. For instance, the average Japanese housewife is not yet liberated from the bondage of the "family," while the average Japanese man is likewise unliberated from the "family" in that he has not given up the idea of exploiting the "family" system to his (the man's) advantage. Of course, there are some people who have solved the problems of the family both in theory and in practise. But there are a greater number of people who are suffering under their own inability to solve the problem in practise, though they have consciously tried to solve it; and there are also a great number of people who live enslaved by the feudal tradition without even realizing the fact. These different levels of emancipation—including, at one extreme, the utterly unliberated, and, at the other, the totally emancipated—exist, not only among different people, but also within the soul of a single person. These various elements that exist among the audience, combined with the various elements of the *Kabuki* itself, create the total complexity of the problem of the *Kabuki* drama. In such a complicated situation, it is incredibly difficult to distinguish the evil effects of feudalism in the *Kabuki* from its good humanitarian effects. It is absolutely necessary, therefore, that the plays and the methods of production of the traditional *Kabuki* drama should be re-examined. It has, indeed, often been attempted, but a more thorough, a more scientific, re-examination of the *Kabuki* is necessary as the first step in re-creating it to live in the present day.

By sifting the various elements of the *Kabuki*, we may arrive at some suggestion as to what kind of new play should be written for *Kabuki* actors to perform. There are actually many " new " *Kabuki* plays—that is, plays written by contemporary playwrights. However, a new play which is merely well suited to *Kabuki* actors cannot answer the question of what should be done about the *Kabuki* drama. It should be a play that would contain some ideas that would appeal strongly to the people of today; and, at the same time, it should be suitable not for the realistic presentation of the modern drama, but should be most effective when presented with the traditional *Kabuki* technique of exaggeration of expression. No such plays have yet been written; but only when they are written can the *Kabuki* drama live as a contemporary drama.*

The birth of such plays, however, is still not an ultimate solution for the problem of the *Kabuki* drama; for there will still remain the strange situation of having two entirely different groups of actors, the *Kabuki* actors and the modern drama actors. A very long period will be required for the Japanese drama to reach the stage where the same actor will be able to play in a classical play and in a modern play. I believe, however, that Japanese drama should aim ultimately at bringing about a phase of development in which that would be possible.

---

* Editor's note—Junji Kinoshita, who wrote this chapter, has made some experimental efforts in this direction. *The Tale of Hikoichi,* one of his plays based upon Japanese folk-tales, which was originally written for modern drama actors, was produced by *Kabuki* actors on the *Kabuki* stage. This was estimated by some critics to have served to open up a new vista for the *Kabuki* performance. He also wrote a play *Yuki Onna* (The Snow Woman) primarily for *Kabuki* actors, and this was also produced on the *Kabuki* stage.

# Chapter VII

# *Cultural Interchange*

## *Contribution of the* Kabuki *to the World Theatre*

Of all the books on the *Kabuki* written by foreigners, those written by Elisséeff in French and by Kinkade in English are considered representative. These books are historical studies of the *Kabuki*; and emphasis is laid on its exoticism. The writers look upon the *Kabuki* with a kind of nostalgia for the past, rather than treat it as a living subject of the present day.

One example of the influence of the *Kabuki* play on Western plays is found in John Masefield's *The Faithful*. The motif of the play was evidently taken out of the *Kabuki* play *Chūshingura*. The method of dramatic presentation, however, shows rather an influence of the operetta *Mikado*. That is to say, Masefield's play is written from a standpoint far removed from that of the peculiar *Kabuki* technique of dramatic presentation. The heroine of David Belasco's play *Chō-chō-san*, on which is based *Madame Butterfly*, the famous opera having Japan for its background, reminds one of the *Kabuki* in the way the play ends with the self-sacrifice of the woman; but the technique of presentation, and the dramatis personae also, are again entirely different from those of the *Kabuki*.

The Japanese drama *Kabuki* has often been confused with Chinese drama, and also with the *Noh* drama, from which the *Kabuki* developed, and which still survives in Japan. George Jean Nathan, a representative American drama critic, discusses, in his article on the Japanese drama, not the *Kabuki* but the *Noh* drama. *At The Hawk's Well* written by the Irish dramatic poet William Butler Yeats follows the form of the *Noh* drama; and *Light and Darkness* by the French dramatist Paul Claudel is a dramatic poem into which the Japanese dance has been adopted.

The first, and very likely the last, instance of a *Kabuki* play produced by a first-rate foreign producer was the production of the twentieth century *Kabuki* play *Shuzenji Monogatari* by Firmin Gemier in Paris.

In the twenties, a Japanese troupe called the Tsutsui Troupe toured America and Europe, and they were taken to represent the Japanese *Kabuki*. This troupe, hastily organized for a world tour, was quite successful in many countries, and even a well-known European drama critic of the time wrote an article on the *Kabuki* presentation after seeing its performance. The performance by this troupe, however, was simply a *Kabuki* performance turned into a revue: it was the sort of entertainment which might be given side by side with jugglery at a fair. A German critic said it was perhaps a mere imitation but still gave the essence of the *Kabuki* form of presentation. It may have appeared to him as a kind of faubism, or an abstract. The fact that the Tsutsui Troupe had been entirely unknown in Japan proves that it had little intrinsic value, and it clearly had no connection with the real *Kabuki*.

The only instance when the *Kabuki* went abroad with the purpose of performing for the *etranger* was in the summer of 1928 when a troupe composed of first-rate *Kabuki* actors were invited by Soviet Russia to perform at a theatre in Moscow. The *Kabuki* has not traveled even to neighboring Asiatic countries; in Japan itself, it is hardly ever possible to see a good *Kabuki* performance except in a few large cities. The Moscow performance of 1928, therefore, was an epoch-making event in the long history of the *Kabuki*.

The most important event in the history of the *Kabuki*, however, is considered to have been the first visit by the Emperor to the *Kabuki* in the Meiji era. This event helped raise the social position of the *Kabuki* in Japan, and the influence of that one event has been felt in many ways ever afterwards. For a while, the *Kabuki* lost part of its attraction because it attained a greater dignity. This phenomenon, how-ever, did not last very long. Making the drama seem a part of society was indeed a remarkable effect of the event.

One would think the visit to Moscow in 1928 would have left a still greater influence on the *Kabuki*. Indeed, it seems very strange that no great change was brought about in the *Kabuki* through this experience. How the *Kabuki* was received when it revealed its whole aspect to the world, how it was criticized, and what new ideals it absorbed—these things should have had a great significance in the development of the *Kabuki*. Soviet Russia of the time, which had newly emerged as a cultural nation, received the *Kabuki* troupe as national guests, and they seem to have endeavored to praise them highly. But Soviet Russia had her own peculiar point of view in cultural criticism. For instance, the criticism in the *Pravda* on August 26, 1928, said:

" There is of course no question about the drama ' *Kabuki*' being a truly fine achievement. But it is fine in the same sense that a romantic historical movie depicting mediaeval castles and the leaders of faked up wars between feudal lords is fine. We, however, have done away with those things . . . . Some people say it is necessary to distinguish between form and content. How is it possible to distinguish between the two? It is possible only in the dramatic performances restricted to one social class—the repertories of the mediaeval guild of diamond polishers, for instance, which possessed a complete combination and a perfect harmony in spite of the fact that in them the two were distinguished. Thus, it is essentially the form, rather than the content, which is our enemy. . . . The populace of Moscow can learn absolutely nothing from the *Kabuki*."

On the other hand, we find criticisms that are almost too favorable. Lunacharsky says: " The art of the actor has achieved the highest development in Japan. It is a perfected art of the highest order. . . ." Abiv says (in the *Eclan*): " In the *Kabuki* the content of the drama itself is conceived of only as a means for artistic presentation. The position the content of the drama itself holds in the *Kabuki* is apparent from the fact that the playwright's name is never printed on the program." Again, S. Eisenstein (of *The Art and Life*), having studied closely the performances of the *Kabuki* troupe which visited Moscow, argues in part as follows:

" Can one milk a he-lamb? . . . No such art is known to the practises of farming villages. We often say, ' That fellow produces neither wool nor milk—he is of no use whatever.' But even he has a name which he has faithfully earned and some function which should be respected.

Alas, however, our critical vanguard will not look at things in such a way. The most remarkable phenomenon of the theatrical art—the *Kabuki*—has been brought to our country. The most noticeable point in which the *Kabuki* differs from the dramatic presentation of our country—if there is such a point—is the complete unification of the *ensemble*. To the Japanese, sound, action, space, and voice do not accompany each other, nor do they parallel each other; they combine and co-operate as elements of equal significance. . . . It reminds one of football, which is the most collectivistic of sports. The grandeur of the *Kabuki* comes from its art of subsumption, which is different from accompaniment.

It is the subsumption of the fundamental objectives of the

function of one material and another, of the realm of one
'stimulus' and another.   In the *Kabuki*, we 'hear the action,'
and 'see the sound.'   As the voice does not sing the notes,
the hand has to present them!   This is presented with the
accompaniment of sounds from behind the stage and we are
mesmerized by the sublime perfection."

The *Kabuki* troupe which performed in Moscow
and Leningrad was disbanded in spite of invitations
from many other European countries.   Thus the
*Kabuki* has never set foot elsewhere in European
countries.

One difficulty about the Kabuki is that it cannot
show its full intrinsic splendour unless it is performed
in a theatre and on a stage specifically constructed for
it.   It is not impossible to perform a *Kabuki* play in
an ordinary playhouse.   But to have it performed in
a *Kabuki* theatre is like putting fish in water.   The
*Kabuki* is a classical drama form, in which the effect of
the performance facing the footlight and the audience
is specially estimated and emphasized, and the *Kabuki*
performance is constructed and organized on that
foundation.   The analysis of the beauty of the *Kabuki*
made by Eisenstein is also based on this mutual relation between the audience and the dramatic performance itself.   In the *Kabuki*, one might say the stage is
the whole of life.   No character in the *Kabuki*
carries on his back a whole social background, like
the hero of a modern drama.   What is seen on the
stage, what is acted, explained, or told there is the

whole of life. For that reason it was necessary to invent the *hanamichi* by which a character could show the audience what happened before he reached the stage. When the *Kabuki* is confined to the proscenium arch with the fixed frame of a modern Western theatre, the performance becomes very weak. To reconstruct a theatre for a *Kabuki* performance, to provide it with a front curtain that can be drawn to one side, to install a revolving stage, to build a *hanamichi* to run through the audience, and to provide means by which actors may rise onto the stage from under it—all these are no easy matter. But it is very difficult to produce the full splendour of the *Kabuki* unless the theatre has these things which are different from the apparatus of an ordinary theatre.

The Second World War brought Japan to the full notice of the whole world. The culture of Japan, especially the peculiar works of art which had been cultivated, loved, and preserved by innumerable generations through Japan's long history were recognized and advertised as a new discovery by the people who found themselves obliged to spend many years here for occupation work after the War. The *Kabuki* came to be studied as a unique dramatic art, and at the same time it came to attract the attention of foreign specialists. The *Kabuki* technique of dramatic presentation which had remained practically the same for the last 400 years was brought anew to the attention of the

— 149 —

world. Dramatists such as Bernard Shaw, Jean Cocteau, and Nowel Coward had seen the *Kabuki* when they had visited Japan, but they had made very little comment beyond a few remarks of courtesy. The new interest in the *Kabuki* aroused after the war, that is, after the beginning of the second half of the twentieth century, seems to be of a different category from that of the past. Truly earnest studies of the *Kabuki* by foreigners, therefore, will perhaps be made in the future.

Americans' interest in the *Kabuki* has been manifested in various ways. Joshua Logan (in the *Vogue*, August 15, 1952) says: " The elaborate stage devices such as the trap-doors and the huge revolving stage were invented and were being used while we were signing the Declaration of Independence." Indeed, the Americans who have come to Japan after the War have had a tendency to be impressed or taken aback by the strength and tenacity of history and tradition in many Japanese institutions. Certainly America is a young country. In Japan, one may easily find ordinary home furniture, utensils, and works of art that are two hundred or three hundred years old, and they will not even be considered antique. There are, indeed, many Japanese who think that the lack of freedom caused by the tenacity of tradition in Japan is a serious weakness of the country. They think it would be easier in some cases to make progress by destroying tradition rather than by attempt-ing to utilize it.

A foreign dramatist once criticized young Japa-nese dramatists, saying it showed nothing but in-dolence on their part that they did not have the enthusiasm to create a *Kabuki* drama which would be new and unique in the world by utilizing all the material that they had—the invaluable and interesting drama form of the *Kabuki*, the background of a race and a tradition that are so old and colorful. It was none other than Paul Green, the author of *In Abraham's Bosom*, who said it. His opinion sounds very rational. To create a new *Kabuki* drama, a drama that would appeal to the present-day world, it would be necessary to absorb subject matters that would be significant in the contemporary world.

It is possible to analyse the peculiar *Kabuki* tech-niques which have been created during its long history and to apply them to other forms of dramatic presenta-tion. For instance, the exaggerated *Kabuki* technique of presenting joy and anger, grief and pleasure, may be used in a production of a Western drama. The *Kabuki* laughter, with the voice rising and falling, can be quite effective in a realistic dramatic performance. The whole *Kabuki* play, however, like the classical operas, is bound by its form. And the form of the *Kabuki* is immutably fixed in its every aspect. To know the form is to know the *Kabuki*. And if the form is used, it inevitably follows that the play will be further and further removed from the realistic drama and its content.

Demands are constantly voiced for new *Kabuki* plays. And about ten new plays are actually written each year and duly produced, but they are nearly always failures, and they may only contribute to lowering the quality of *Kabuki* performances. It is natural, therefore, that some people should hold that the *Kabuki* should be preserved as pure classical drama, that it should be kept, so to speak, in a glass case of a museum. The *Kabuki* drama, however, is a living thing, breathing, moving, and even self-criticizing at times; and it is no easy matter to discover a means by which it may be preserved in a glass case.

Now, to make out what manner of living thing this *Kabuki* is, it may be better to quote from an article written by a person who has come from across the ocean to see the *Kabuki* for the first time, rather than to refer to any Japanese in whose blood runs the essence of the *Kabuki*. James A. Michener, the author of *South Pacific*, writes in *Holiday*, August, 1952:

"*Kabuki* hit me like a thunderbolt. Far to the left sit two men, one with a musical instrument, one with a book from which he sings in a weird, high, wailing voice. Now the stage fills with actors dressed in fantastically rich costume. Then comes a shock, for they start to speak and they sound like nothing ever heard before on earth. In unbelievably cruel distortions of the human voice they throw sounds to the top of the balcony. At first the *Kabuki* voice is appalling but soon it weaves an intense dramatic spell. It sounds like Japan centuries ago : harsh, unearthly, powerful. From the back of the theatre a curtain is ripped aside and down a runway leading to the stage walks a woman. When she speaks it is as if all the cats in hell had been let loose. The voice is a piercing cry that rises and falls at least two octaves and sounds like a distant siren in the wind. No woman is allowed to act in *Kabuki.* . . ."

No Japanese could possibly think of using such words in describing the *Kabuki*. Still, we cannot deny that they do describe the *Kabuki* : we can only agree and admit, with a grim smile, that the *Kabuki* would in truth give a foreigner such an impression. If we evaluate it philosophically, if we wake out of our mesmerized state, we realize what a strange drama it is, and what strange techniques of presentation are used in it. And yet we cannot deny the fact that it is precisely the strange part of the *Kabuki* that sustains its peculiar form. A woman who is not a woman and yet leaves us no doubt of her being a woman—that is where the *Kabuki* begins. The queerness cannot be removed. It must be evident how difficult it is to write a new *Kabuki* drama now. It must also be evident that it is very difficult to put present-day life and society into a surrealistic *Kabuki* performance.

There are many people who have studied the history of the *Kabuki*. But one often encounters difficulty in finding adequate literary sources for scientific proof of various phases in the development of the *Kabuki* which has existed for the masses, while on the other hand treasures and buildings over a thousand years old have been preserved intact, protected from fire and dampness. Thus, in many cases, we have only the assumption based on a popular, or generally accepted, view. For instance, at the beginning of a dance drama called *Okina*, which is always performed on important congratulatory occasions both in the *Noh* and the *Kabuki*, there is a famous line which goes, " *Tō tō tarari. . .* ," which no one has been able to construe. One theory is that it was part of a Dharani song sung at festivals in ancient Tibet. There are, indeed, many questions concerning the origin of the *Kabuki*, and its historical development, and probably new discoveries are yet to be made, like the recent discovery that brought new doubts about the works of Molière. The questions still unsolved in the *Kabuki* seem to be much greater. Whatever questions there may be concerning its historical development, the form of presentation itself has remained a solid inheritance from old days. In Western drama, the written drama is handed down to posterity as literature, or a form of dramatic presentation is inherited as one phase in the history of drama. The *Kabuki*, however, has been handed down through the ages to the present day by human beings, through their physical bodies. In this respect, it is undoubtedly a unique drama in the world.

A book titled *Japanese Theatre*, written by Faubion Bowers, has recently been published. It discusses the origin, the history, the plays, the esthetics of the *Kabuki*, simply following the popular conceptions of the *Kabuki*. Containing also synopses of a few plays, it is a kind of introduction to the *Kabuki*, written in English. It boasts of no new discoveries or remarkable arguments. Still, the writer expresses the following anxiety in a chapter titled " Reality versus Unreality ": " There is in general much which prevents an actor from achieving realism in *Kabuki*. There are too many basic and traditional inconsistencies. If they were resolved, *Kabuki* would end up as a plain modern theatre performed on a hopelessly incongruous base, and its deep esthetic delight would vanish."

It is necessary to realize that tradition, particularly a long tradition, is a tenacious thing. Any attempt to change or to bring about further development in the traditional art of the *Kabuki* in the present second half of the twentieth century would be accompanied with great difficulty and would very probably end in complete failure. For the *Kabuki* has already become an art that lives in the past. The *Kabuki* lived in each generation and developed little by little until it was perfected; but it is clearly no longer possible for it to live with the changing world, now or in the future.

In other words, it can never become a modern play. It can only live in its own tradition; and though it may acquire greater width, so to speak, it cannot grow deeper; neither can it advance. On the other hand, since it is warmly preserved, unconsciously, in the blood of the Japanese people, as an inherited tradition, no attempt to destroy it could easily succeed. The inherent power of this tradition can be proved by the fact that even an elementary school child, when taken to the *Kabuki*, is sufficiently impressed by what he feels directly through his body—even if the content of the play is not understandable—to move his limbs, grieve, and rejoice in unison with the action on the stage.

Does this mean then that the *Kabuki* form of dramatic presentation can in the future merely be preserved and valued for its unique quality, but cannot develop in any single aspect? I can conceive of no development for the *Kabuki* itself. However, it has great possibilities as a potential influence on other dramas. In the past, the *Kabuki* had a significant influence upon the *Ukiyoe*. And the Japanese *Ukiyoe*, carried over the seas, had great influence on Western painting, as, for instance, on Van Gogh. A similar influence may be given by the *Kabuki* itself. We need not perhaps confine its possible future sphere of influence to foreign dramatics. Just as the *Ukiyoe* was digested and absorbed into the spirit of Van Gogh, the *Kabuki* may offer a key to a development in dramatic presentation in other forms of dramas, either in Japan or in foreign countries. Such a contribution would ultimately mean a development and a growth of the *Kabuki* itself.

*Index of Japanese Words*

# INDEX